A Kid's Guide to
KEEPING CHICKENS

Melissa Caughey

Storey Publishing

The mission of Storey Publishing is to serve our customers by
publishing practical information that encourages
personal independence in harmony with the environment.

Edited by Deborah Burns and Lisa H. Hiley
Art direction and book design by Jessica Armstrong
Indexed by Nancy D. Wood

Illustrations by © James Gulliver Hancock
Cover and interior photography by © Keller + Keller Photography, except for, © Adam Mastoon, 18 (middle left), 19 (bottom left and right), 21 (middle right); © Amy Kerk/iStockphoto.com, 18 (top right and middle right), 19 (top center); © Blend Images/Alamy, 98 (right); © Cheryl Barnaba, 19 (top right); © Custom Life Science Images/Alamy, 20 (top right); © Danakia/iStockphoto.com, 29 (top left); © Daydreams Girl/iStockphoto.com, 20 (bottom right); © Debbi Smirnoff/iStockphoto.com, 19 (bottom center); © Edward Westmacott/iStockphoto.com, 21 (bottom right); © Mars Vilaubi, 14; Mars Vilaubi, 20 (bottom left), 27, 67, 69, 115; © Folio Images/Alamy, 22 (bottom); © Gerald Lacz/FLPA/Minden Pictures, 20 (top center); © GlobalP/iStockphoto.com, 40 (center and right), 41 (left); © HedgehogWhisperer, 20 (top left); © Life on White/Alamy, 40 (left); © Linda Steward/iStockphoto.com, 21 (top right); © Melissa Caughey, 119 (bottom left); © Paul Rapson/Alamy, 22 (top); © Petro Perusky/Alamy, 41 (right); © picturesbyrob/Alamy, 49 (top); © Sally Smith/Alamy, 18 (top left); © Sarah Rowland/FLPA/Minden Pictures, 20 (bottom center); © Simone Van Den Berg/Dreamstime, 19 (top left); © Studio Annika/iStockphoto.com, 29 (all but top left and bottom right); © Tom Scrivener/Alamy, 98 (left); © Valerie Garner/Alamy, 99; © wescott/iStockphoto.com, 21 (top left)

LIBRARY OF CONGRESS CATALOGING-IN-PUBLICATION DATA

Caughey, Melissa, author.
 A kid's guide to keeping chickens
/ by Melissa Caughey.
    pages cm
  ISBN 978-1-61212-648-7 (hardcover
with pull-out poster : alk. paper)
  ISBN 978-1-61212-418-6 (pbk. with
pull-out poster : alk. paper)
  ISBN 978-1-61212-419-3 (ebook) 1.
Chickens—Juvenile literature. 2. Eggs—
Production—Juvenile literature. I. Title.
SF487.5.C38 2015
636.5'1—dc23
                          2014033788

Storey Publishing
210 MASS MoCA Way
North Adams, MA 01247
www.storey.com

Printed in Canada by Transcontinental Printing
10   9   8   7   6   5   4   3   2   1

To my own chicks,
Jacob and Madeline

CONTENTS

ACKNOWLEDGMENTS

First and foremost, I would like to thank my family for their love and support throughout this entire process. Thank you to my husband, Peter, for his willingness to always pick up a pen and reread this book a million and one times. Thank you to my children, Jacob and Madeline, whose energy, ideas, and spirit embody this book. Thank you to Tilly and the rest of our feathered family.

Thank you so much to all the supporters of Tilly's Nest and my endeavors over the years. I am so lucky to have you all along on my journey. Thank you to Dawn at Treats for Chickens for all your help in the kitchen. You are my chicken soul sister. Thank you to Pam and Alexis at Sensational Silkies by Blake for teaching me so much about showing chickens. Thank you to my dear friend Lauren for believing in me and this book. Thank you to all of my chicken friends who let me photograph their beautiful coops, yards, and creativity in the garden. Thank you to Barks and Bubbles for sharing their natural pest repellent with us for our dog, Sara, and now our chickens.

A special thanks to all the kids whose photos appear in these pages: Shea; Alan and Mia; and Gracie, Madelyn, and Spencer, as well as to the kids who answered my questions about keeping chickens: Aislinn, Alexis, Edison, Haddie, and Xavier. I'd also like to thank photographer Joe Keller and his assistant, Jeff Stiles, for taking such wonderful pictures.

Thank you to the entire team at Storey Publishing who helped me to create this beautiful book. And last but not least, a special thank-you to my amazing editors, Deb Burns and Lisa Hiley, and art director, Jessica Armstrong, for believing in me and helping to make this book a reality.

ADVENTURES IN CHICKEN KEEPING

If someone had told me 10 years ago that I would move across the country from Los Angeles to Massachusetts and take up backyard chicken keeping, I probably would have told them that they were crazy. Why in the world would a city girl like me do such a thing? Well, I did move to Cape Cod and I soon realized that I was constantly spotting chickens and their paraphernalia. I saw chickens at our local pick-your-own farm and roaming in people's yards.

Then a friend invited me to meet her flock: a colorful group of about 20, including a vibrant rooster, hens with poufy headdresses, and hens with speckled feathers. After my tour of the coop, her run, and the entire setup, I was smitten. With a gentle nudge from my friend, who offered to take my chickens in case it didn't work out, I placed my order. Six chicks were delivered to our doorstep just in time for the kids' summer vacation.

We could not get enough! We sat in the garage on a beach blanket peering into the brooder for hours. We watched them sleep standing up. We watched them become best friends with the digital thermometer. We enjoyed their interest in the newspaper photo that they unearthed while scratching in the shavings. We just fell in love with our six little fluff balls.

Several years later, chickens have become an integral part of our family life. We have laughed, cried, said goodbye, and learned so much. The chickens have helped us reevaluate our lives. Somehow our vegetable garden has tripled in size. We have taken up beekeeping. We plan our vacations around our chickens. After a long day, we look forward to relaxing with the hens. We worry about them as we do about our dog. I knew my husband had finally come to love the flock too when he came in one evening after locking them up and told me, "You know, I really would miss those girls if they were gone."

This book shares the adventures that my children have experienced with our backyard flock. We have discovered that not a day goes by without the chickens making their way into our daily activities. I hope that this book will not only inspire you to keep a flock of your own but also inspire you to take time and spend some quality moments with your family.

As you embark on your own journey, you will quickly discover that there are many ways to provide food to your flock, supply water, house them, and raise them. The best advice that I can give you is to do what works best for your climate, your backyard situation, and your lifestyle. Oh, and one word of warning — chicken keeping can be very addictive!

Melissa

1 WHY CHICKENS?

Most folks begin keeping chickens primarily for the eggs. Why wouldn't you want a pet who can deliver breakfast to you every day, no matter what the weather?

And with their bright, electric-orange yolks and perky egg whites, fresh eggs can't be beat. Eggs from your own chickens taste better and are healthier for your body. But as people begin to explore the idea of keeping chickens, they find other reasons why chickens are great.

For one thing, you don't need much room to have a couple of hens. Chickens take up very little space, and whether you live in a big city, the suburbs, or the lush countryside, a small flock of hens can be tucked away anywhere. A small chicken coop can fit into practically any yard. Chickens are easy to care for and require a minimal amount of attention. Chicken-keeping supplies are readily available at feed stores, as well as at many hardware stores and also online.

Chickens are also part of the local food or *locavore* movement, which is sweeping the country in response to consumer demand for locally produced food, sustainable farming practices, and more self-reliance. As more and more people want to know where their food comes from, and want to be able to grow as much of their own food as they can, farmers' markets, pick-your-own farms, and restaurants that use local ingredients are becoming increasingly popular.

But there's another reason that so many people are jumping on the chicken bandwagon — these birds are just plain fun to have around!

TREATS FOR YOUR FLOCK

Jell-O Summer Party Treat

Who doesn't love Jell-O on a summer day? Well, chickens are no exception. They'll gobble up this easy-to-make treat filled with protein and goodies that you add just for them. Have fun experimenting to see what your flock likes best!

INGREDIENTS

  4 packets unflavored gelatin
½ cup apple juice
  1 cup cold water
2½ cups boiling water

Mix-in Ideas
Chopped hard-boiled eggs
Cracked corn
Dried mealworms
Fruit and vegetable peels
Oats
Sunflower seeds

1. Spread the mix-ins into a square cake pan (a silicone one releases the mixture easily).

2. Combine the gelatin, apple juice, and cold water in a bowl.

3. Carefully add the boiling water. Stir until the gelatin is completely dissolved.

4. Pour the liquid over the mix-ins and mix well.

5. Put the dish in the refrigerator to set for 3 hours.

6. Cut into pieces before serving to your flock.

More than Just Eggs

I first started thinking about getting chickens when my kids were little. They wanted a dog; I wanted a pet that did not require quite as much attention. We had just moved to a place where we could garden, and I wanted to show them how to plant vegetables and harvest a crop, and to share with them how valuable the land can be. I also wanted them to understand that producing food isn't as easy as it seems. At the time, they thought that if you wanted eggs, you could just head down to the supermarket. In reality, each egg is a gift that takes time and effort to produce.

Chickens and kids seem to go hand in hand. We soon learned they make wonderful pets. Each one has her own personality. We had no idea how much fun they could be! Our hens recognize us. They nuzzle with us and sit in our laps. They love to be petted, like a dog or cat. They can be trained. They are capable of emotions. They form a family in which each bird has her own role. They have their own language and communication techniques.

LIFE LESSONS

Our chickens have taught us many basic lessons. They remind us about love, patience, acceptance, camaraderie, and compassion. We have learned about the circle of life: saying goodbye, witnessing new life, caring for those with handicaps, and so much more. Our birds are such wonderful teachers that we call living with them going to "chicken school," and you'll see boxes throughout this book that tell about what we've learned from them. But that's not all!

Chickens work hard from dusk until dawn, helping keep your yard free from insects such as ticks. They enjoy dining on weeds and scraps from the kitchen. Their manure can be turned into the most amazing compost, which in turn nurtures the garden. Another wonderful thing about keeping chickens is spending more time outside. We all enjoy gardening for ourselves and for the chickens.

WHY I LOVE CHICKENS!

AISLINN, Age 8, Pescadero, California

How long have you been keeping chickens?
I have had my own chicks for about a year.

What do you love about keeping chickens?
They are pretty easy to care for and they are the type that don't care what you say. You could call them your best friends. Pluses: Chickens are easy to care for, they can be tamed easily, they are funny, and they are sometimes more smart than you think. Minuses: They aren't *always* smart, it can be trouble cleaning out their habitat, and all chickens can peck but usually chicks' pecks don't hurt at all.

Do you have a favorite breed and why?
I like bantams. They are a little breed and inspire nurturing care in kids.

What is your favorite thing about chickens?
I like being encouraged and inspired by chickens. They are bold and brave, and good friends to anyone who's willing to be brave, too. I think that pretty much sums it up.

Do you have any advice for other kids just getting started?
My best advice is, don't underestimate a chicken! When they try doing something and they fail . . . well, I would keep an eye on them for the rest of the week. Just one more ultra-important question: ARE YOU READY FOR THIS?!

Before You Begin

If you are like us, the most fun is choosing the types of chickens you want to have, but first you need to think about all that is necessary for keeping chickens. Chicken housing should be at the top of your list. Chickens need a dry, safe place to take shelter from bad weather and predators. Chickens also require care and attention — not a lot, but you can't neglect them!

They need fresh food and water daily, and the coop needs some light housekeeping each morning and a good cleaning now and then. You will need to collect eggs a couple times per day, too. Chicken keeping requires a responsible and dedicated owner.

One of the most important things to take into account when planning for chickens is the amount of space that you have for your flock and where they will live. Anyone with a little bit of space can raise chickens, but you must keep your space and living conditions in mind when you select your breeds. If you live in the country, your flock can have more space. If you live in the city, your chickens will most likely be confined to their coop and an outside run most of the time.

Some breeds handle confinement well. Other breeds do better when allowed to roam free. The important thing is to provide enough space so that the living areas do not develop odors, the chickens don't fight, and everyone is healthy and thriving.

Chickens spend a lot of time in their coop and run. The coop is their housing, and the run is the fenced-in area that allows the flock access to the outside.

HOW MUCH SPACE?

A standard-sized chicken needs a minimum of 10 square feet of space to live comfortably. The coop should provide 2 to 3 square feet of that total, with an additional 8 or so square feet in the run. Bantams need 5 to 7 square feet per bird.

As an example, a flock of four standard hens should have 8 to 12 square feet of coop space and at least 32 square feet in their run. A coop that is 3 feet wide by 4 feet long (12 square feet) allows for 3 square feet per chicken. A run that is 4 feet wide by 10 feet long (40 square feet) will provide adequate space for a flock this size.

It is always best to give your flock as much space as you can, especially if they will spend most of their time confined to the coop and run. In colder climates, where chickens spend more time indoors in poor weather, a larger coop might be a good choice. In warm climates, where the flock can spend more of its time outdoors and use the coop only for laying eggs and sleeping, a smaller coop works just fine.

PLANNING AHEAD

Another important thing to keep in mind is how long your chickens will live. Chickens typically live anywhere from 5 to 7 years, but some can live as long as 20 years. Hens lay the most eggs during the first couple of years, but after that, egg production tapers off and becomes more sporadic. When egg production dips, some people choose to find a new home for their entire flock and begin again with young chicks in the spring.

Other folks keep their aging chickens and add new chicks to the flock, which means increasing their living space. As you figure out space requirements for your initial flock, you might want to factor in a little extra room just in case you decide to add to your flock later.

LOCAL LAWS & ORDINANCES

Before you get too excited about chickens, take some time to research whether you are legally able to keep them in your town. Some towns have strict rules and regulations. Some have guidelines about the number of chickens you can have. Some have limitations on keeping roosters. Others require you to keep the chicken coop a certain distance away from property lines, buildings, neighbors, and so forth.

Please use your common sense and be a courteous neighbor. For example, figure out how to prevent your chickens from wandering into neighbors' yards without permission. Keep your chicken coop clean and take good care of your birds.

Eggs are a wonderful way to connect with your neighbors — sharing a gift of eggs can make even a wary neighbor curious and supportive about your backyard chickens.

DAILY CHICKEN CHORES

You may be surprised to hear that chickens require just a little of your time each day. I estimate that all of their daily needs can be provided for in less than 20 minutes a day!

For the most part, your flock will wake up each morning and return to the coop at dusk. On your days off from school or during summer, you can mix up your routine. It won't bother the flock one bit!

But always remember that they can't take care of themselves, so it is very important that you (or someone you trust) check on your flock every single day. When you go on vacation, you'll need to plan ahead.

Before you go away, talk to a friend or neighbor who can take over while you are away. Make sure they know the whole routine. Many people are happy to help out because of the fresh eggs they can take home!

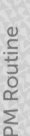

AM Routine

GOOD MORNING!

The chores start when you let the chickens out of their coop into the run.

FILL FEEDER

While they stretch their legs, top off the feeders as needed.

PM Routine

FREE TIME!

If you let your flock free-range, this is a good time to let them roam.

FUN WITH YOUR FLOCK

Spend some time just hanging out with the hens or make them a special treat.

CHECK WATERER

Chickens need plenty of fresh, clean water.

LOOK FOR EGGS

Take a peek to see if any of the hens have been busy.

TIDY UP COOP

Scoop out manure, if necessary, before your day's adventures.

CHECK FOR MORE EGGS

Check for afternoon eggs. There might be some late layers!

TIME FOR BED

As it gets dark outside, make sure all the chickens are safely inside the coop.

LOCK UP TIGHT

You don't want any predators sneaking into the coop at night.

Learning about Chickens

What is the best way to do your research before you order your flock? A poultry show is a terrific place to start and lots of fun to go to. Poultry shows happen throughout the year all over the country (a search on the Internet should turn up a few near your home). At almost any show, you'll find many different breeds and plenty of owners who are willing to "chat chicken."

Don't feel shy — just be friendly and ask questions. Look for kids like you who are showing their birds at the event. Most chicken owners are happy to share their experiences and tell you why they fell in love with a particular breed.

QUICK CHICK FACTS

Female chickens are called *pullets* for the first year of life, then they are called *hens*.

Male chickens are called *cockerels* for a year before they are called *roosters*.

Hens start laying eggs at five to six months of age. The larger the breed, the longer the wait for eggs.

Hens lay the most eggs during their first two years of life.

Chickens live an average of five to seven years with proper care.

When you can't find a chicken show in your area, here are some other places to look for information.

→ **The Internet.** While you must be careful about the material you find online, plenty of good resources are available. One of our favorites is My Pet Chicken. This site has a breed selector tool to help you narrow down your selections. You put in the qualities you want, including egg color, weather-hardiness, number of eggs, and even personality, and it suggests the best chickens for your family.

→ **Your library.** See if your community library or school library has any books on getting started with chickens. This might be a great way to do some of your required school reading, too. Who knows, you might even convince some of your classmates or your teachers to think about adding a flock to their backyards!

→ **A local feed store.** Many feed stores sell baby chicks in the spring, so the folks there will probably be excited to help you start up a new hobby. They can let you know which breeds they are ordering and direct you to all the necessary supplies.

→ **Other backyard chicken keepers.** You might be surprised to discover that your classmates, family friends, or neighbors have already embarked on the chicken-keeping journey. Most would be happy to share all they have learned about their flock, their coop and run setup, and some great tips to get you started.

ANATOMY OF A CHICKEN

Some chicken body parts are the same as a human's (even though it's hard to see their ears!), but some are very different. And some have funny names like "wattle" and "hackle." It's a good idea to become familiar with the parts of a chicken.

uropygial (preening) gland

comb

ear

eye

earlobe

nostril

beak

tail feathers

wattle

hackle

back

cape

crop

vent

wing

hock joint

scale

toe

shank

spur

web

feet

claw

2 CHOOSING THE BEST CHICKENS

Once you begin to investigate chicken keeping, you will quickly discover many breeds to choose from. When we first started out, we had no idea that so many types of chickens existed!

Frankly, it can be a little overwhelming, and if you are like most kids, you will want to meet and keep every single chicken breed. Certain breeds, however, do work better in certain situations.

What should you consider when beginning to select your flock? Most people use these criteria when picking out their breeds:

→ Needs of the breed based on climate

→ Personality of the breed

→ Number of eggs laid per week and their color

→ Feathering and color

→ Size of full-grown chickens

Some people want to raise their own chickens to serve at the family table, and some breeds are better suited for that purpose than others. This book is more about chickens who are going to be family pets, not Sunday supper.

Where Do You Live?

Where you live plays an important role in which breeds you select. Chickens have been bred to tolerate various climates all around the world. Heat-hardy chickens are best suited to live in warm climates, and cold-hardy ones do well in places that have snowy, freezing winters. If you live in the desert, you will need chickens who can tolerate warm weather. We live on Cape Cod, in Massachusetts, so we keep all cold-hardy breeds.

It may seem strange, but chicken coops do not need to be heated in the winter. Placing a heat lamp or two near dry, combustable tinder such as pine shavings is a setup for disaster. In climates where winter temperatures regularly dip below freezing, you can insulate your coop to help keep your flock warm. In very hot climates, you need to pick a partly shady spot for the coop and cover portions of your run to provide shelter from the sun. Some chicken keepers even add fans to keep their flocks cool.

Chickens are birds, not mammals like us. Their bodies handle changes in temperature quite differently than ours do, because they have higher body temperatures to begin with. Their feathers help regulate their body temperature, allowing them to tolerate colder temperatures than we can.

Another difference is that their lungs work more efficiently, and they have larger hearts compared to mammals of the same size. If you select breeds that are suitable for your climate, you should not have any problems with them adapting to your backyard.

FEATHERS & FLUFF

All chickens have feathers, of course, but the variety of types, shapes, and colors is amazing — and on just one bird! Like eggs, feathers are made of protein, so a good diet is important for healthy, shiny feathers. Different types of feathers have different jobs, as described below.

WEBBED FEATHERS cover the wings, tail, and most of the body for protection from wind and rain.

DOWN FEATHERS (or plumules) grow next to the skin and provide warmth.

BRISTLES are found around the eyes, nostrils, and beak. They protect against dust and pests.

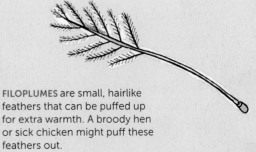

FILOPLUMES are small, hairlike feathers that can be puffed up for extra warmth. A broody hen or sick chicken might puff these feathers out.

Pick a Nice Chicken

We think a hen's personality is far more important than what she looks like or what color eggs she lays. We started keeping chickens when Jacob was only six years old and Maddy was three, so it was important to choose breeds that would be comfortable being picked up and handled by the kids. We wanted chickens who would come to us when we would call them and who would follow us around the yard.

Fortunately, plenty of breeds are known for their friendly personalities and mellow natures. Just be aware that even if you pick breeds that tend to be docile, it is not a guarantee for each individual bird. Each has its own personality. (See Top 10 Breeds for Kids, page 18.)

Green Eggs? Sure!

One of the most wonderful **rewards** of having chickens is collecting the eggs. Such a great feeling comes from heading out to the nesting boxes in the morning and lifting the lids to discover those warm little orbs of goodness. Most chickens lay three to five eggs per week. The eggs can be beautiful, too. Easter Eggers lay eggs in light hues of pink, green, and blue, and there's a breed called Copper Marans that lay chocolate-colored eggs!

The color and size of the egg are basically the same in all chickens of the same breed, but each hen lays a specific size, tint, and shape that are the same during her entire life. We can tell which chicken has laid which egg. This observation comes in handy because you can tell when certain chickens are not laying eggs and you can investigate the reason why.

CHICKEN SCHOOL

Beauty Is on the Inside

Our dear Silkie, Dolly, is usually bald. Whenever she goes broody, which is about every three weeks, the other hens peck at her head to tell her to leave the favorite nesting box, but she stays put, even if they peck her head clean of feathers! This has happened so many times that I don't think her fluffy topknot will ever return normally. She'll probably always look a bit silly.

But Dolly is beautiful in so many other ways. She is one of the sweetest and gentlest chickens ever. She loves to sit in our laps, being petted and talked to. We often hear her clucking and cooing, as though communicating to newly hatched chicks. She is friendly to all her flock mates, and will join another broody hen in the nesting box even when she is not broody herself!

People prize birds for their plumage, but the color or appearance of their feathers does not matter to the chickens themselves. It doesn't matter if they have no head feathers, are walking around with a messy bottom, or have mites or poultry lice. They are still a flock, and at night they can be found nestled closely on the roosts, sleeping side by side.

WHY I LOVE CHICKENS!

EDISON, Age 14, Ashtabula, Ohio

How long have you been keeping chickens?
Seven years.

What do you love about keeping chickens?
The enjoyment of having birds around — I love birds.
I love the personalities of the different breeds.

Do you have a favorite breed and why?
I can't really choose a favorite — I love them
equally for different reasons. The Cochins are so
affectionate and funny. The Polish have unique
personalities, and they have different clucks and
sounds for communication. The d'Anvers are small
and easy to handle but have big personalities.

What is your favorite thing about chickens?
I like to watch them digging and scratching and just being
birds. That's when you can see their personalities come
out. Our Cochins come running up to us looking for
treats — it's fun watching those little fluff balls running.

**Do you have any advice for other kids just getting
started?**
Go to poultry shows to look at all the different breeds
and varieties. Talk to the judges and breeders to
see what type will fit with your goals the best.

15

TYPES OF CHICKEN COMBS

Combs help chickens regulate their body temperature. Cold-hardy breeds tend to have smaller combs, which are less vulnerable to frostbite. Heat-hardy birds usually have larger combs that can release more heat. Chickens also recognize one another by their combs.

Here are some common comb shapes and breeds that have them (turn the page to learn more about these breeds).

SINGLE
Australorp
Barred Rock
Buff Orpington
Cochin
Faverolle

PEA COMB
Brahma
Easter Egger

V-SHAPE
Polish

WALNUT
Silkie Bantam

ROSE
Wyandotte

Check Out That Chicken!

Of course, we are all drawn to the particular look of one breed or another. Some of these birds are really beautiful! Some have poufy topknots; others have feathers streaked with an array of colors. Some have yellow feet, some have black feet, and some have feathered feet. Their combs and wattles (those fleshy appendages on their heads and under their beaks) come in all sizes and shapes.

You can choose a flock of chickens that all look alike, or you can have fun picking out different breeds to make up your flock — it's up to you!

QUICK CHICK FACT

To be a *purebred*, a chicken has to have two parents of the exact same breed. With mixed breeds, two different breeds are used to form a different type of chicken with certain characteristics. For example, Ameraucanas are crossed with other breeds to produce Easter Eggers, which lay multicolored eggs. Mixed-breed chickens are sometimes called *barnyard mutts*.

Standards versus Bantams

Chickens come in a couple of different sizes. Standard chickens grow to about the size of a large house cat and weigh anywhere from 7 to 10 pounds when fully grown. They can be an armful to pick up. Bantam chickens are smaller, about the size of a small bunny or guinea pig, and weigh 3 to 5 pounds. They are easier to handle, making them perfect for smaller children. Our Silkie Bantams are so lovable and easy to handle that we always let first-time chicken holders carry one of them around first.

Of course, smaller hens do lay smaller eggs! Two bantam eggs equal one standard egg.

If you are looking for very big birds, then check out the Jersey Giants. They are some of the largest chickens available in the United States. The hens grow to more than 10 pounds and the roosters are usually more than 13 pounds!

You can mix bantams with standard-sized hens, and you can also mix the breeds. This Silkie Bantam and Buff Orpington live happily with other hens of various breeds.

My kids love to fry up bantam eggs for breakfast . . .

. . . because it's more fun to have two eggs on toast than one.

TOP 10 BREEDS FOR KIDS

Here are the 10 chicken breeds that we have found work well for families and tend to be the most docile, friendliest birds. By no means does this list include all the possible breeds: There are hundreds of different ones out there! You can always do more research to find out about breeds that aren't included here.

Silkies are unusual in several ways. One is having blue earlobes!

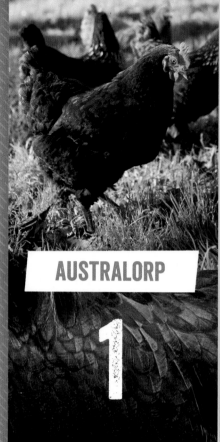

AUSTRALORP

1

→ This Australian breed has black feathers that shimmer iridescent green in the sun. As the birds age, sometimes the tips of their feathers become a bit speckled with brownish gray.

→ These hens often establish themselves at the top of the flock.

→ They are homebodies and handle confinement well.

→ This breed is curious, friendly, and outgoing.

→ Hens lay about five medium-to-large brown eggs every week.

PLYMOUTH ROCK

2

→ These chickens were developed during the nineteenth century in New England and continue to be popular in the region.

→ They are standard-sized chickens known for living a long time.

→ They are gentle creatures who do very well with people and get along with other pets.

→ They lay four or five pinkish-brown eggs per week.

→ The Barred Rock, shown here, looks a little like a zebra with its black-and-white striped feathers.

BRAHMA

3

BUFF ORPINGTON

4

COCHIN

5

→ Brahmas come in both standard and bantam sizes.

→ These chickens are friendly, not skittish, and trainable and are good birds for children to show. They do not mind being handled, and even the males are a bit more docile than other breeds.

→ They come in a variety of colors.

→ They have feathers on their feet.

→ The hens lay lovely brown eggs approximately three times per week.

→ These chickens are the golden retrievers of the chicken world.

→ Originally from England, they are large, friendly birds with golden feathers.

→ They are curious and incredibly lovable, and they enjoy being held.

→ They handle confinement to the coop and run well.

→ They can go broody (see page 30), and typically lay three large brown eggs per week.

→ Cochins, like Silkies, originated in China.

→ These fluffy-feathered chickens even have feathered feet. Some have frizzled (curly) feathers.

→ They come in eight different colors and both standard and bantam sizes.

→ They can adapt to living in a coop for their entire life but also free-range well.

→ They are a quiet, friendly, hardy, and very calm breed.

→ You might expect three brown eggs per week.

EASTER EGGER

FAVEROLLE

POLISH

6

7

8

→ If you want colored eggs, then you'll want a couple of these hens. Their appearance can vary, but they carry a genetic trait that means their eggs can be tinted in hues of blue, green, olive, and pink.

→ This is not an official breed but a type of chicken. They come in the standard size as well as bantam.

→ Easter Eggers get their ability to lay colored eggs from either an Araucana or Ameraucana parent, but the other parent can be another breed.

→ These are friendly, curious birds.

→ They lay approximately four eggs per week.

→ These French chickens stand out by having five toes instead of the usual four, fluffy cheek feathers (called *muffs*), and a feathered beard.

→ They come in a variety of colors; the most popular one is salmon.

→ These chickens don't mind being confined to the coop and run.

→ They are incredibly docile, making them particularly suitable for younger kids.

→ They lay about four light brown or creamy eggs per week.

→ This is a friendly breed with an unusual look.

→ Some people say that this breed's poufy head feathers can cause issues, such as problems with their vision and feather picking from the other hens. The feathers can be gently trimmed to help with vision, and if Polish chicks are raised with other breeds, problems usually don't arise.

→ Polish come in standard and bantam sizes.

→ They are not the most reliable egg layers. If you are lucky, you can expect two white eggs per week.

SILKIE BANTAM

9

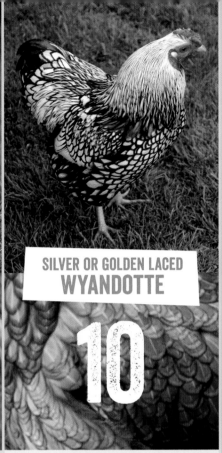

SILVER OR GOLDEN LACED WYANDOTTE

10

What about the Rhode Island Red?

Rhode Island Reds are a very popular breed. They are wonderful egg layers and are incredibly hardy. They can also be docile and calm.

However, some people find that this breed can be aggressive toward other chickens. A harmonious henhouse is important, which is why Rhode Island Reds do not make this Top 10 list.

This doesn't mean that you shouldn't consider them, though. They might be just what you're looking for!

→ This ancient breed was first described by Marco Polo on a visit to China in the thirteenth century.

→ They are tiny, lightweight, and easy to handle, and they have a few unusual features. The most noticeable is that their feathers, which come in many colors, are fluffy instead of smooth.

→ They also have five toes (most chickens have four) and black skin (instead of yellow).

→ They tend to go broody a lot (see page 30), so this is not a breed to depend on for eggs.

→ The eggs are about half the size of standard eggs and range from cream to white in color — some even have a slightly pinkish tint. When a hen is laying, you can expect about three eggs per week.

→ These incredibly beautiful birds were developed in the United States.

→ They come in many colors, but the Silver and Golden varieties are the most readily available. They have either a white or gold lacing pattern between the black on their feathers.

→ The rose-style comb is perfect for cold regions as it is less prone to frostbite.

→ They are a smaller breed, averaging approximately 6 pounds for the hens.

→ Chock-full of personality, they can be domineering and are typically the head hens in their flocks.

→ They make excellent mothers and lay lovely pale brown eggs four or five times per week.

Can you guess which state claims this breed as its official state bird?

21

Keeping Roosters

As you learn about chicken keeping, you will surely read that keeping roosters (male chickens) stirs up controversy. Roosters can't lay eggs, but they do serve three purposes: they protect the flock, help keep order among the hens, and fertilize eggs to make chicks.

You do not need a rooster to have your hens lay eggs, but you do need a rooster to have the eggs hatch.

It is not necessary to keep a rooster with a flock of hens, however. Hens are perfectly capable of defending themselves and sorting out their relationships, and they will lay eggs just fine on their own. But if you want your hens to hatch out their own chicks, you will need a rooster, and some people enjoy having them around.

Roosters are fun to watch. They show off for their girls with a dance in which they shuffle their feet and drag their wings on the ground. They share food with the hens by picking up and dropping special treats, a behavior called tidbitting. They are also quite brave; a rooster who notices danger will herd the flock to safety and then come out to face the predator. He might even sacrifice his life for his hens.

TOO PROTECTIVE?

Because they are so protective, however, they can be aggressive. When a rooster perceives danger or competition for his girls, he may chase, peck, and dig his spurs into whomever he interprets as a threat, and that can include you, your friends, and your pets. If you have more than one rooster, each should have at least seven hens of his own to protect; with fewer hens available, roosters will fight with each other and may try to mate too often with the hens.

Some people end up with roosters accidentally, either from hatching their own chicks or from a mistake at the hatchery. The hatch rate is exactly the same for males and females, 50 percent. If you decide to hatch or incubate your own eggs, approximately half of them will be males and grow up to be roosters. Have a plan for what to do with those extra roosters.

TREATS FOR YOUR FLOCK

Crispy Treats

My kids love making marshmallow-rice treats on rainy weekends. One day they asked if we could make them for the chickens and this recipe was born. Try placing one of these treats into an outdoor bird suet feeder.

INGREDIENTS

2 cups puffed rice or wheat cereal (sugar-free)
1 cup cracked corn
1 cup sunflower seeds for birds
½ cup water
¾ cup flour
1 packet unflavored gelatin
3 tablespoons honey
Cooking spray

1. Lightly coat the bottom of a 13-by 9-inch pan with cooking spray.

2. Mix the cereal, corn, and sunflower seeds in a bowl.

3. Whisk together the water, flour, gelatin, and honey in another bowl.

4. Add the dry ingredients to the wet ingredients and mix them all together with your hands.

5. Pour the mixture into the baking pan and spread it evenly.

6. Cut into four even pieces.

7. Allow to dry and harden overnight before giving it your flock.

3 FINDING YOUR FLOCK

One of the most important things to realize about keeping chickens is that they are very social birds. In order to thrive, they need company.

I always tell people who are starting out that four chickens is the smallest number they should keep, and those should all be hens. With four hens, your flock would still number at least three should something happen to one of your birds. With a small flock, it's easier to introduce new members.

A flock of four is about the perfect size for a family of four. That number should supply you with about a couple dozen eggs per week. Of course, don't be surprised to find yourself wanting more chickens. Chicken keeping can be addictive!

It's exciting to have new chicks arrive in the mail from the hatchery.

Which Comes First?

After you have decided on the chicken breeds you want and figured out where you will house them (see chapter 5 for information on building a coop), you need to figure out how to obtain your chicks. You have several options. The most common are to purchase chicks from a local feed store or to order them from a hatchery. In either case, have your brooder ready for their arrival. (See page 36 for tips on how to set up the brooder.)

You can also hatch fertilized eggs in an incubator, or once you have grown hens, you can let them hatch a clutch of chicks (see page 30 for more about that). Discuss with your parents the best way for your family to start on your great chicken adventure.

BUYING CHICKS FROM A FEED STORE

The easiest way to start out keeping chickens is with a visit to your local farm supply or feed store. Ideally, the store will have a few breeds to choose from, but typically you won't have as many options as you would from a hatchery. By late winter, the feed store should be able to provide you with a list of chicken breeds that are coming in, when they are expected to arrive, and what the policy is about picking them up. Most feed stores carry baby chicks only until late spring.

Don't mix and match chicks of different ages. Chicks have different temperature requirements at different ages, and older, larger chicks might bully smaller ones.

Unless the feed store ordered a straight run (mixed gender group), you can assume they have ordered all female chicks. Be sure to ask about that, so you'll know what to expect. There is still a 10 percent chance you could accidentally end up with a rooster, but that is the case even when you order from a hatchery.

An advantage to buying chicks this way is that you can select the healthiest-looking or cutest ones from the group. Look for ones who are alert, appear to be eating and drinking, and move about the brooder without any problems. Be sure to ask if they have been immunized.

QUICK CHICK FACTS

A *straight run* means that the chicks haven't been separated by gender, so there will be females and males in the group.

A *sexed run* means that the chicks are either all pullets (young hens) or cockerels (young roosters).

Thinking up names for your chicks is fun. There are so many options!

BUYING CHICKS FROM A HATCHERY

For more than a hundred years, the United States Post Office has transported day-old chicks all across the country. While it's pretty amazing to witness the actual hatching of a chick, it is also a magical experience to welcome a box of tiny cheeping fluff balls to their new home.

Ordering from a hatchery has a few benefits. You can specify females only, and you can select chicks of multiple breeds. You can purchase immunized chicks, which is worth the small added cost.

Chick ordering begins in the late fall, but the babies are not delivered until warmer weather. When deciding when to have the chicks delivered, plan back from the age they will be when you put them outside in the coop — the weather should be not too cold.

Many hatcheries will ship a minimum number of chicks in a single order. Be aware, however, that if they're shipping when temperatures are still chilly, some hatcheries add extra chicks for warmth. Most often these extra chicks are males, which you probably don't want, so ask if the hatchery will add only females. Scheduling delivery for warmer weather might prevent the arrival of unexpected chicks.

What Happens at the Hatchery?

The journey starts in walk-in incubators, where large trays filled with fertilized eggs are rotated regularly. After 21 days, the eggs hatch, and the once-quiet space comes alive with the sounds of hundreds of peeping chicks!

Hatchery workers examine the chicks to determine their gender and immunize them, if requested. Other workers fill the orders, placing chicks into boxes with air holes and nesting material. After the chicks reach their final destination, the post office will call to inform you that your peeping package has arrived. You'll be very eager to see your new babies, but to keep them safe and warm, don't open the box until you are home.

It is important to know that sometimes chicks perish during transit. If you discover a dead chick, inform the hatchery once you've introduced the rest of your chicks to your brooder. (See chapter 4 to learn about raising chicks.)

Once your chicks arrive, inspect each one carefully before settling it into the brooder.

Hatching Chicks from Eggs

Hatching your own eggs is a great experience. It is amazing to watch a chick emerge from its egg, then watch her grow and develop. The process is relatively simple: You need some fertilized eggs, a heat source, and proper humidity levels. You can rely on an incubator to simulate a mother hen. Be prepared for disappointment, though — not all fertilized eggs will produce live chicks (see How to Candle Eggs, page 28).

USING AN INCUBATOR

You can buy an incubator at a feed store or online, or you might be able to borrow one from a friend or nearby farmer. Simple incubators require that you turn the eggs or add water to achieve the appropriate humidity. A more expensive one will automatically turn the eggs and adjust the humidity.

The next step is to find fertilized eggs. The size of your incubator will determine the number of eggs; for good results, leave some space around each one. You can purchase fertilized eggs from a local farmer, breeders, and various online sources. Many breeders will ship fertilized eggs, but the hatch rates can be poor and the egg quality can't be guaranteed. You may have better success with local eggs that you can pick up yourself.

If you follow the directions on your incubator, and all goes well, you should have baby chicks in approximately 21 days.

EMBRYO DEVELOPMENT

It's amazing to think that a fertilized embryo develops from a tiny speck into a baby chick in just 21 days.

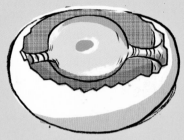

DAY 3

DAY 5

DAY 10

DAY 20

HOW TO CANDLE EGGS

After the eggs have been in the incubator for about a week, you should check to make sure the embryos are developing properly. Not every embryo will become a live chick, and you'll need to remove those eggs from the incubator. Candling, or shining a light through the shell, is a simple and very cool way to see what is happening inside.

- A flashlight
- A 4- by 4-inch piece of cardboard
- An empty toilet paper roll
- Scissors and tape

→ **ON DAY THREE,** a fertilized egg has a blood spot.

→ **AT SEVEN DAYS,** you can see the red amnion (the sac that holds the embryo) and the vasculature (veins and arteries) that nourishes the growing chick.

→ **AFTER TWO WEEKS,** the chick is taking up so much room that the light can no longer shine through.

What You Do

1. Cut a hole in the cardboard square that is slightly smaller than the opening of the toilet paper roll.

2. Center the roll over the cutout and tape it into place. Secure the cardboard device to the flashlight with tape.

3. Examine the eggs one at a time. Before you take them out of the incubator, number each egg in pencil so you keep track of them.

4. Turn on the flashlight and hold the egg on the tube.

The Hatching Process

Hatching from its egg is the most difficult work that the chick will face in its whole life. Just prior to hatching, the chick absorbs the remaining energy from the yolk sac that has nourished its growth. This energy reserve allows the chick to survive for three days without food or water after hatching.

Important: It may be tempting to help the chick break free, but you are more likely to hurt it than help it, so keep your hands away and just watch.

QUICK CHICK FACTS ?

→ It can take up to 24 hours for a chick to hatch fully.
→ Interfering with the hatching process can actually hurt the chick.
→ Baby chicks have an energy reserve and don't need food or water for the first couple of days.

The chick makes a tiny pip hole with a special egg tooth on its beak, which falls off within a few days of the chick hatching.

Over several hours, the chick uses the egg tooth to hammer a fine crack around the shell, starting at the pip hole.

During this process the chick will nap off and on.

Once the crack is completed, the chick begins to push the egg apart with its feet. It struggles to emerge from the cramped place where it has been growing.

Wet and exhausted, the chick sleeps quite a bit at first.

The chick's feathers soon dry and fluff up. In just a few hours, it begins to explore its surroundings.

Using a Broody Hen

Another way to successfully hatch eggs is to use a hen that will "go broody," if you have one. Broodiness is a natural mothering instinct that makes a hen want nothing more than to hatch her eggs and raise her chicks. Over the years, farmers who wanted hens to lay eggs instead of hatching chicks have deliberately bred this trait out of many breeds because when hens are broody, they are still eating, but they aren't laying eggs. Some breeds, like Silkies, still have a tendency to go broody.

A broody hen has some very distinct behaviors. She will lay an egg almost every day for about 10 days. At first you will be amazed at how productive she has become. Soon, however, you will find her spending almost her entire day in the nesting boxes. Despite your attempts to shoo her away, she returns almost immediately, determined to sit in the box with or without eggs.

A broody hen also removes all of her chest feathers to create a broody patch. She places this bald patch of skin directly against her eggs to keep the temperature and humidity just right. As she sits upon her nest, she spreads out her wings and flattens her body to snuggle as close as possible to her eggs. She is protective, murmuring a low growl to keep others away.

She comes off her nest only once or twice a day to eat, drink, and evacuate her waste. By the way, broody poops are the worst — extra big and super stinky!

THE RIGHT KIND OF EGGS

If you want to let a broody hen hatch some eggs, you need fertilized ones. If you have a rooster, you can assume that all the eggs your hens lay are fertile. Or you can purchase fertilized eggs as you would for an incubator. Broody hens do not discriminate. Their only instinct is to hatch those eggs and be a mother to those chicks.

If you are waiting for fertilized eggs, let your broody hen sit on a few unfertilized eggs in the meantime. Once the fertilized eggs are available, number each one with a pencil. Let them rest on the kitchen counter for 24 hours prior to placing them underneath your broody hen to allow them to arrive at room temperature.

Place an odd number in the nest, as the eggs fit together like a puzzle that way. Once the fertilized eggs are placed under your broody hen, they should hatch in approximately 21 days.

MAKING A BROODY BROODER

Create a brooder (see chapter 4) just for your hen and her clutch to keep the other hens away. They may break her eggs out of jealousy or steal her clutch from her. Even after she's been sitting on the eggs for weeks, another hen might swoop in and kick the broody hen off the nest, then hatch and claim the baby chicks as her own.

A brooder also allows you to monitor the hen and her chicks carefully. When the chicks are growing, you can easily control the brooder's temperature and keep the chick feed separate from the rest of the flock. (It is okay for a broody hen to eat the same feed as the chicks.)

Finally, though it very rarely happens that a broody hen is not interested in raising her chicks or even tries to harm them, with a brooder you can remove her and keep the chicks safe.

OUR BROODY ADVENTURE

When we first started keeping chickens, we accidentally ended up with a Silkie rooster. After he became a bit aggressive, we gave him to a farmer friend. Knowing that we had fertilized eggs, we decided to hatch a few in the hope of replacing him with a couple of female chicks. We had no idea how amazing this journey would be.

Our Silkie hen Dolly goes broody so reliably that we call her our "growling pancake," so she was a natural choice to brood our eggs. We created a brooder from a small chicken coop inside our garage. We lined the bottom of the run with cardboard and pine shavings and made a nest in a small square cardboard box full of shavings.

We transferred Dolly and her eggs to the nest and gave her a small feeder of food and a waterer. It was February, so we placed a heat lamp in the brooder with her. There she sat in her Zen-like broody state for 21 days.

Each day we removed Dolly from her eggs so she could stretch her legs and wings, defecate, and reacquaint herself with her flock. This was important so that she would maintain her position in the pecking order. Her visits were brief, limited to 15 minutes. We developed a

routine. When the time came to return her to the nest, I would call out, "Eggs, eggs, eggs." She would waddle on over, satisfied to return to her eggs. And so it went, day in and day out for her entire broody period. In spite of the cold, the kids loved spending time in the garage with Dolly.

Then one morning, I heard the eggs peeping. I reached under Dolly to take a peek at the eggs. Some had tiny pip holes in them from the egg teeth. The chicks were hatching!

That afternoon, Jacob had a friend over. They sat, waiting, watching for something to happen. Dolly talked to her eggs. She cooed to them. She coached them. Finally, the kids shouted from the garage, "Hurry, the eggs are hatching!"

We witnessed the first little baby push her way from the egg. Wet and tired, she collapsed from exhaustion. Dolly gently nudged the chick

with her beak, moving her to safety underneath her body.

Over the next 24 hours, the remaining eggs hatched successfully. Dolly raised them all beautifully. She cared for them and taught them everything they needed to know about being a chicken until they were ready to explore the world on their own.

After about five weeks, her work as a mama hen was done. She lost interest in her babies and resumed laying eggs.

QUICK CHICK FACTS

→ Most broody hens will instinctively create a clutch that is an odd number of eggs.

→ A bantam hen can sit on approximately 9 eggs, while a standard-sized hen can sit on 15.

A CHICKEN FORT

It is always nice to have a place to hide away from the world — a secret place in the yard where the world seems to melt away, where you are content to sit with a chicken in your lap just hanging out. We have one such place in our backyard, a place where some 20-year-old rhododendrons form a tiny alcove, perfect for two little people and a couple of chickens. Old stumps turn into stools, and an old blanket makes things cozy.

Creating a chicken fort in your own landscape is easy with a little imagination. If you don't have a hidden spot already tucked in the landscape, you can make a simple tepee with fast-growing edible vines. The chickens will linger a bit longer if your fort has edible vines and vegetables as incentive for frequent visits. They might even like the fort so much that free-ranging hens take to laying their eggs inside.

CHICKEN-FRIENDLY VINES
→ Cucumbers
→ Nasturtiums
→ Squash
→ Zucchini
→ Hops

TOXIC VINES
→ Beans
→ Peas
→ Morning glories

WHAT YOU NEED
- Measuring tape
- A ladder
- Posthole digger
- 7 (6- to 8-foot-long) bamboo or steel rods
- Spray paint
- Gardening wire (large gauge) or rope
- Garden netting/trellis netting, made of heavy-duty nylon
- Climbing vines
- Burlap (optional)

What You Do

1. In a flat, sunny location in the yard, map out and spray-paint a circle with a 6-foot diameter.

2. Divide this circle into eight sections, as you would a pizza, and mark them off. Determine where the entrance will be and put an X on that spot so you know not to dig a hole there.

3. With the posthole digger, dig a hole at least 18 inches deep at each marked-off section.

DIG DEEP!

TIE TIGHTLY!

4. Place a bamboo pole in each of the seven holes and backfill with soil. Tamp them down well so the poles stay in place.

5. Gently bend the tops of the bamboo supports toward the center of the circle.

6. Secure the tops of the bamboo together with gardening wire or rope.

7. Wrap the support rods with garden netting for climbing vines around the tepee, leaving the entrance uncovered.

8. Plant vines around the base of the tepee, avoiding the entrance, and train them to grow up the fort's walls.

9. Water the vines well as they grow. Within a few weeks (depending on what you plant), your fort will be a great little hideout.

If you prefer a more instant fort, cover your chicken fort with burlap or jute fabric, instead of planting vines. A large flat rock works for a table, and a few tree stumps serve as furniture.

FROM CHICK TO CHICKEN THE FIRST SIX WEEKS

After you determine which breeds you would like to raise and know when they will arrive at your home, it's time to make a temporary home for your chicks. For the first six weeks, before you move them to their permanent coop, they need to be in a sheltered place where you can keep a close eye on them.

Depending on when your chicks are scheduled to arrive, you need to take temperature into consideration, both indoors and out. Your chicks' lives will depend on a warm, safe, and draft-free environment.

If you are ordering chickens in very early spring, keep them inside the house, in a bathroom or spare bedroom. If you are ordering chicks later in the spring or early summer, then it might be fine to keep them in your garage. One thing to think about is that baby chicks make a lot of dust and peep quite a bit!

Birthday Cake

We might be crazy, but we think chickens deserve something special once in a while. We make this cake for the flock every year, and we even sing "Happy Birthday." Sometimes we have to divide the cake onto two separate plates because certain members of the flock forget their manners when they see it!

INGREDIENTS

¼ cup flour
¼ cup water
4 tablespoons creamy peanut butter
½ teaspoon baking powder
1 small apple, diced
3 strawberries, diced
Butter for baking sheet
⅓ cup plain yogurt
Raisins or scratch
Fresh herbs

1. Preheat the oven to 350°F/175°C.

2. Mix together the flour, water, peanut butter, and baking powder until well combined.

3. Add the apples and strawberries and mix well.

4. Grease a baking sheet with a bit of butter and place the dough on the sheet. Form the dough into a circular shape about 1 inch thick with your hands.

5. Bake for approximately 20 minutes. Remove from the oven and cool.

6. Transfer the cake to a plate with a spatula. Top the cake with yogurt for frosting, raisins or scratch for sprinkles, and fresh herbs or fruit for decoration.

How to Make a Brooder

The first step in creating your chicks' temporary housing is to make an enclosure. It should be at least a couple of feet high to keep the chicks from escaping. It must be draft-proof, as chicks can become chilled in even the slightest breeze, but have good ventilation. It needs a cover to keep predators out — your pet cat might be very interested in those chicks! Use a piece of hardware cloth, which is like chicken wire but sturdier and with smaller openings, or an old window screen, secured in place with bungee cords.

You can make a brooder out of all kinds of materials. Some people cut down a large cardboard appliance box. Some use a big plastic storage bin or an old 20-gallon aquarium

A safe alternative to a heat lamp is an EcoGlow Chick Brooder, which comes in two sizes and doubles as a perch!

(these can be heavy, but they work fine). If your family is handy, you can build one from scraps of lumber. Or you can buy one at a farm-supply store or on the Internet. A cardboard box is the cheapest and often the most convenient container, but always consider the possible risk of fire from the heat lamp.

In addition to the container, the most important item is a heat lamp to keep the chicks nice and warm. The heat lamp should have a ceramic socket and a reflective metal dome. It needs to be adjustable so you can move it closer or farther away as the chicks' temperature needs change.

Many heat lamps use an infrared bulb that produces red light, but it becomes very hot very quickly. The red light deters the chicks' natural tendency to peck at everything around them, including each other, by making everything appear to be red. You'll just need to check carefully that the light isn't close enough to the container to start a fire.

The heat lamp also comes with a clamp; however, using the clamp alone is not enough. If the lamp is jarred loose, it could fall into the brooder, possibly harming the chicks and potentially starting a fire. It's much safer to fasten the lamp with a bungee cord in addition to the clamp.

If the outside temperatures are already pretty warm, especially in late spring or early summer, you may find that the heat lamp, no matter the adjusted height, keeps the brooder too warm. If this is the case, try switching out to a regular lightbulb to keep the brooder in the proper temperature range for the chicks.

BEDDING FOR THE BROODER

Chicks need proper bedding in the brooder. Bedding not only provides a soft place for the chicks to rest while sleeping but also serves to keep the brooder dry from droppings. I find that kiln-dried pine shavings work the best. For the first couple of weeks,

We think watching chicks is more fun than watching TV!

QUICK
CHICK
FACTS

Here's what your brooder temperature should be as your chicks grow:

Week 1 95°F (35°C)

Week 2 90°F (32°C)

Week 3 85°F (29.5°C)

Week 4 80°F (26.5°C)

Week 5 75°F (24°C)

Week 6 70°F (21°C)

Week 7 65°F (18°C) – chicks can move outside!

line the brooder floor with cardboard and scatter about two inches of pine shavings over it. Tidy the shavings daily by scooping out the poop and any wet clumps where chicks have been having too much fun in the waterer. Replenish with some dry shavings. Keeping the brooder clean and dry is a main key to having healthy chicks.

As the babies age, they will learn how to naturally roost when they sleep. Providing branches as makeshift roosts helps them transition to sleeping off the ground.

Chicks in the Brooder

For the first few weeks of life, chicks need to stay very warm without becoming overheated. If the brooder becomes too hot or too cold, the chicks could become ill or stressed, or even die. The temperature inside the brooder during the first week should be 95°F (35°C).

To determine the temperature, place a digital thermometer in the center of the brooder floor where the heat lamp shines. As each week passes, decrease the temperature by five degrees.

You will know immediately if your chicks are happy with the temperature. If they huddle together directly underneath the heat lamp, then they are too cold. If they hug the edges of the brooder and avoid the heat lamp, then they are too hot. If they wander freely about the brooder, eating and exploring, then the temperature is just right.

At six weeks of age they will be fully feathered and should be able to stay warm on their own as long as the temperature does not dip too low below 60°F (15.5°C).

Add some marbles or rocks along the rim of the waterer to prevent drowning if a chick happens to fall asleep with its head resting on the rim.

FOOD AND WATER SETUP

Local feed stores carry an assortment of chick-sized feeders and waterers. See chapter 6 for more information on what chicks need to eat. Chicks make a mess of any type of feeder as they scratch through the shavings and run around the brooder.

Putting the feeder on a piece of cardboard can help keep shavings out of the feed. I also recommend placing the waterer on a brick after the first week or so to minimize spillage and pine shavings in the water from rambunctious chicks.

THOSE CHEEPING, CHARMING CHICKS

There's nothing cuter than a bunch of fluff balls running around the brooder cheeping and hopping. After they've been eating and exploring for a while, you can see their little eyes getting heavier and heavier and then they just suddenly flop over, sound asleep!

Like all babies, chicks need a lot of sleep as they grow, so when they are napping, leave them alone. Save your handling time for when they are awake and active and looking for fun. Or let them take a nap in your lap — that's fun, too!

Sometimes a chick (or even all of them!) will fall asleep while you're holding it. You can let it take a little nap on your lap or very carefully put it back in the brooder.

Time to Move Outside

Once the flock reaches six weeks of age and overnight temperatures are consistently at least 60°F (15.5°C), then your flock is ready to move outside. Make the transition first thing in the morning when you can spend an hour or two with them. You want to be certain they don't get into any trouble that you didn't foresee when you constructed the coop. You might prefer to allow the chicks to adjust to the inside of the coop for a few hours before allowing them access to the run.

You will need to play tour guide for your chicks. The most important thing is to show them where their food and water are. Be sure they can see and reach both. At first, you may need to scoop them up from the run in the evening and place them on the roosts, then lock them in for the night. Remember that their world just got a lot bigger, and sometimes they need a bit of tender loving care from their human family.

WHAT'S THAT IN CHICK YEARS?

Over the course of six weeks, your fuzzy little chicks will transform from fluffy babies to awkward adolescents to mini adults. Here's what you can expect.

1 DAY (INFANT)

- 100% fluff
- Egg tooth still on beak
- Sleeps most of the time

5–7 DAYS (PRESCHOOLER)

- Wing feathers appear
- Spends more time exploring

2 WEEKS (MIDDLE SCHOOLER)

- Starts to perch
- Tail feathers sprout
- Can fly out of brooder

CHICKEN SCHOOL

Being Brave

Fifi, one of our Silkie bantams, is a loner. She is at the bottom of the pecking order. She is curious, but also a bit timid, and tends to keep to herself. Most evenings, she sleeps alone. She sometimes hangs out with the other Silkies, but most of the time, she explores life alone.

I used to feel badly for Fifi and would worry about how to make sure she had a good quality of life, but one morning, I thought, "Could Fifi just be brave?"

After all, she is healthy and thriving, even if she spends most of her time on her own. She isn't being picked on, and she happily scratches in the garden. She gets plenty of treats and affection from us.

Fifi marches to her own drummer, and that seems brave to me. Being brave isn't always easy. It can be scary. It might mean being different, or not doing what everyone else is doing.

Watching Fifi inspires my kids to be brave. They've learned that you just have to stretch your neck out and explore the world on your own.

4 WEEKS
(TEENAGER)

- Goes through a scruffy, scrawny phase
- Lots of feathers coming in
- Comb and wattles becoming more pronounced

6 WEEKS
(YOUNG ADULT)

- Fully feathered
- Still growing
- Ready to move outdoors

5 MAKING A HOME FOR YOUR HENS

I'm pretty sure your parents won't let you keep a grown chicken in your bedroom (although you can buy diapers for indoor chickens, believe it or not). For one thing, chickens can be pretty messy, even messier than kids!

For another, chickens are actually happier living outside, as long as you provide them with a clean, safe coop with enough room for each hen to stretch her wings. The coop is the chickens' house, where they sleep and lay their eggs and hang out in bad weather.

The run is their yard — it's an enclosed outside space where they can exercise and scratch around for bugs. They can move between the two during the day, but they should be locked into the coop at night.

In chapter 1, we talked about how much space you need to keep a small flock, and now we'll look at what kind of housing and fencing you need to build. You'll find as many styles of chicken coops as there are kinds of people houses, but the good ones all have the same characteristics: they are safe, dry, and comfortable.

Seed Rolls

In the wintertime, we like to make seed rolls for the wild birds and the chickens. This fun treat encourages chickens to peck at something else besides one another.

SUPPLIES

Garden twine
Scissors
Empty paper towel or bathroom tissue rolls
Butter knife
Creamy peanut butter
Cracked corn
Seeds: chia, buckwheat, sunflower, millet, and sesame
Plate

1. Cut a piece of garden twine approximately 3 feet long. String it through the cardboard roll and tie it off in a knot. Spread a thin layer of peanut butter over the entire roll.

2. Mix the corn and seeds together, then pour some on a plate. Roll the tube in the seed mixture.

3. Hang a couple of them inside the coop or outside in the run for hours of entertainment.

Selecting the Perfect Spot

When selecting the best place for your chicken coop, first review your local laws. In addition to observing those requirements, be considerate of your neighbors. Be sure to follow the guidelines for setbacks and the proper distances from other buildings and property boundaries.

The spot should be level and flat, with good drainage — not a place where water collects in puddles. It should receive some sun during the day to help keep things dry but should have some shade as well. It should be visible from your home, so you can check on your flock from a window. Don't forget to consider ease of access, which is especially important if you live in a place where it snows.

This small coop with a moveable run is situated at the edge of a driveway near some trees, where it is sheltered from bad weather but can easily be seen from the house.

Coop Design

Some coop and run setups are permanent, while others have wheels and can be moved to new locations. The movable models are called chicken tractors (some have wheels), and they can be constructed to hold flocks of all sizes. The most important thing about the coop is that it be weatherproof. In addition to being in a dry location, it should be sturdy enough to stand up to strong gusts of wind. Every coop needs doors with predator-proof latches, a vital feature for the safety of your flock.

Base the design of your coop on the climate where you live. If you live in a cold place, you might consider insulating the coop. If you live in a place with considerable rainfall, a sloped roof is a must. If space is limited, the run can be built partially or entirely underneath the coop. If you love gardening, you can create a living roof made of plants. Coops can have skylights, windows, and other customized features. You can have an open-top run or a covered one that provides shelter for the flock.

You can buy books about building coops, or check them out at your local library, or look online for free plans. You can also order chicken coops that are ready to assemble, or that come preassembled. These can be a bit pricier due to shipping costs. They are heavy. Building a coop takes time and planning, but it keeps the cost down compared to purchasing a preconstructed coop.

People have also converted old doghouses, playhouses, gardening sheds, and so forth into coops. Your only limitation is your budget and your imagination!

FOUR DIFFERENT STYLES OF CHICKEN COOPS

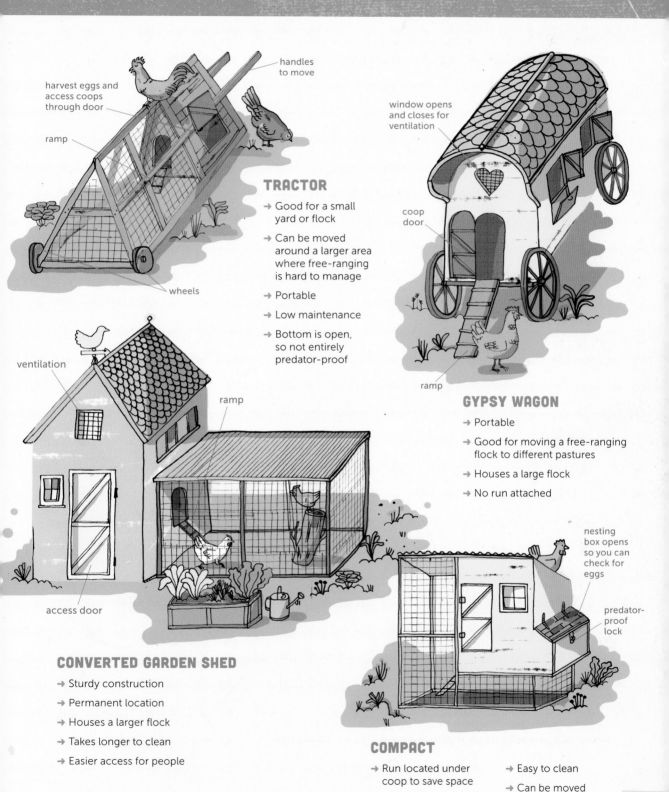

harvest eggs and access coops through door

handles to move

ramp

wheels

TRACTOR

→ Good for a small yard or flock

→ Can be moved around a larger area where free-ranging is hard to manage

→ Portable

→ Low maintenance

→ Bottom is open, so not entirely predator-proof

window opens and closes for ventilation

coop door

ramp

GYPSY WAGON

→ Portable

→ Good for moving a free-ranging flock to different pastures

→ Houses a large flock

→ No run attached

ventilation

ramp

access door

CONVERTED GARDEN SHED

→ Sturdy construction

→ Permanent location

→ Houses a larger flock

→ Takes longer to clean

→ Easier access for people

nesting box opens so you can check for eggs

predator-proof lock

COMPACT

→ Run located under coop to save space

→ Flexible design options

→ Affordable

→ Easy to clean

→ Can be moved

→ Limited space

45

We designed our second coop with plenty of windows to provide ventilation and light. Hardware cloth screens keep out predators.

INSIDE THE COOP

When creating your coop and run, allow approximately 10 square feet of total space per standard chicken and 5 to 7 feet per bantam. Typically, chicken coops have a floor with four walls and a roof. Some look like garden sheds or mini houses.

The coop should be draft-free while having good ventilation. Ventilation is usually provided by a window or vent near the top of the coop. A window that opens and closes is a good idea. The window offers light to stimulate egg production and provides ventilation on warm summer days. The coop and run should have places for a feeder and a waterer, as well as small hanging dishes for oyster shells and grit.

Each chicken should have about two feet of roosting space above the ground. The roosts should be smooth, rounded, and no more than two inches wide. Removable roosts are the easiest to clean. After you clean them, you can place them in a sunny spot to dry.

Lining the nesting boxes and the coop floor with linoleum makes cleaning the coop a great deal easier. It is washable and also extends the lifetime of the coop. Check flooring stores for affordable linoleum remnants (pieces left over after bigger pieces have been cut).

CHICKEN SCHOOL

Home Is Where the Heart Is

We love that our chickens keep us grounded. Some people may believe that you need material things to be happy, but the happiness those things brings quickly fades. In reality, what is important is right in front of you. The chickens remind us that simple is better.

Chickens don't need cell phones, laptops, fancy shoes, or expensive toys. They enjoy an occasional treat, but all they really need is proper shelter and enough food and water. They don't spend all their time texting, watching TV, or playing video games. They like being outdoors,

free to explore. They wake up together every morning, eat together, and roost together.

A home is made with those who care about you. It should be a sanctuary where you are supported, loved, and believed in. It can even be in your heart. Our chickens remind us of the way a home should be.

A PEEK INSIDE

Here's one way to set up a coop — there are plenty of different ways to include these key features.

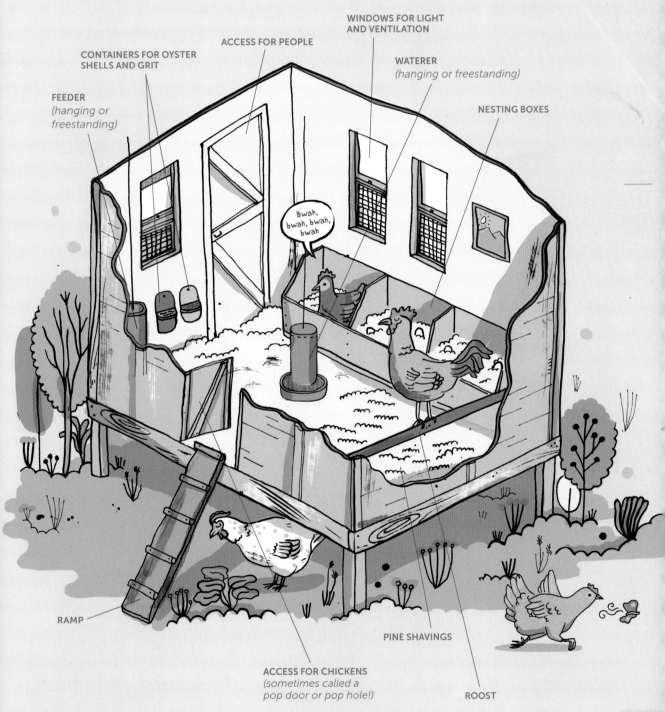

FEEDER
(hanging or freestanding)

CONTAINERS FOR OYSTER SHELLS AND GRIT

ACCESS FOR PEOPLE

WINDOWS FOR LIGHT AND VENTILATION

WATERER
(hanging or freestanding)

NESTING BOXES

RAMP

ACCESS FOR CHICKENS
(sometimes called a pop door or pop hole!)

PINE SHAVINGS

ROOST

Multiple nesting boxes give your hens a choice of places to lay eggs — they often pick a favorite spot.

LIGHTS, ACTION!

Electricity in the coop can be a bonus, although you must encase the wires, because chickens will peck them out of curiosity. Electricity allows you to add lights, fans, and devices to keep waterers from freezing.

Having a light in the winter provides hens with more "daylight," which stimulates their brains to keep laying eggs. This, of course, is optional. We do not light the coop and our hens still lay during the winter, although the number of eggs certainly tapers off.

If you do add a light, put it on a timer, so it turns on early in the morning and turns off when there is still daylight. This way, no chicken is injured if the light suddenly turns off in the evening's darkness when the flock has not yet settled onto their roosts for sleep.

NESTING BOXES

Nesting boxes are safe places where hens lay their eggs. Designs vary, but any box should be approximately 12 inches by 12 inches and filled with nesting material such as pine shavings. Some nesting boxes hang outside the coop and are accessible though a trapdoor that allows you to reach in to collect the eggs.

Whatever the design, nesting boxes should be elevated slightly off the ground. Most people put the nesting boxes in a dark corner, where the hens feel more protected. Some people even craft curtains to provide privacy.

There should be one nesting box per three or four hens. You will probably discover that all the hens like the same nesting box. Our hens have several choices, but we often find them lined up waiting to lay their eggs in one particular nest!

Some chickens develop the bad habit of sleeping — and pooping — in the nesting boxes overnight. This leaves you with dirty chickens and dirty eggs. If you find a chicken prefers spending the night in a nesting box, simply wait until nightfall to scoop her up and gently guide her feet onto the roost. Chickens can't see in the dark, so she'll be easier to handle and won't leave the roost for the night. It might take a few days to retrain her.

Hens shouldn't have nesting boxes until they are at least 18 weeks old. Simply block the boxes off with cardboard until the chicks are all habitually sleeping on the roosts and are closer to egg-laying age.

Your chickens will appreciate having a place to perch in the run.

Building the Run

You know that phrase "all cooped up"? Well, you don't want your flock to feel that way, so your coop needs an enclosed area where your chickens can safely roam during the day. Even if you allow your flock access to your yard, it's a good idea to have a run. There will be times when you will not want them to roam because of predators or bad weather, or when you are on vacation and can't keep an eye on them. Runs are often attached to the coop, but you can build a movable one so that your chickens have access to fresh grass.

Be aware that chickens will scratch up a patch of ground pretty thoroughly, so a permanent run will soon become all dirt inside. Chickens also like to take dust baths to remove bugs and excess oil from their feathers. Some people provide their flock with a large shallow bin full of dirt, wood ash, and sand for a bathing station.

Build your run large enough, with the entire flock size in mind. Most chicken coops, even ones built low to the ground, have ramps leading from the coop into the run rather than a step — it's just a little safer. The run should be sturdy, with a sloped roof if you choose to cover it. Most runs are constructed from lumber and hardware cloth. Some incorporate corrugated plastic sheets or even cedar shakes as roofing.

QUICK CHICK FACTS

Rub-a-dub-dust! To take dust baths, chickens dig shallow holes and lie in them. They wiggle into the ground and use their wings to toss dirt and debris onto their bodies. Sometimes they appear to be doing yoga. Other times, they just relax and appear to have become completely boneless!

CHICKEN JUNGLE GYM

Some friends of ours made a fantastic jungle gym for their flock in their run. It looks like a barren tree and is about 8 feet tall and 5 feet wide.

The chickens hop from branch to branch and take naps perched up high. It's a great place to hang treats, and you could even create a chicken swing with a small branch!

WHAT YOU NEED

- One large, thick branch or sapling, long enough to reach the top of the run
- A number of smaller branches, in varying lengths but at least 2 inches in diameter
- Handsaw
- Branch pruner
- Posthole digger
- Sturdy rope
- 2-inch decking screws (optional)
- Cordless screwdriver

What You Do

1. With help from an adult, trim your support branch, leaving forks where you can attach the smaller branches. Trim off twigs from the smaller branches.

2. Dig a hole 2 to 3 feet deep with the posthole digger and insert the long branch. Backfill the hole with soil. The branch can stand upright or lean at an angle. You can attach the top of it to the run for added stability.

3. Create a structure with the remaining branches, spacing them apart however they fit best in your run. Secure them to the main branch with rope and/or screws.

Predator Proofing

When building your coop and run, it's very important to consider the predators in your area. Not all areas of the country have the same predators, but every area does has animals that would like to eat your chickens or their eggs.

Common threats include snakes, raptors, minks, weasels, raccoons, foxes, coyotes, and fisher cats, and even bobcats or bears. Contact your county's cooperative extension office or your local fish and wildlife department to find out which predators you should watch out for.

Dogs and cats, both domestic and feral (wild), can also be a threat. In fact, pets can be a bigger problem for neighborhood chickens than other predators are, so use common sense when your flock is free-ranging.

Predators operate both day and night, and they are smart. They look for the easiest ways to access the chickens. They can dig into the run, break into the coop, or enter the run from overhead. Rats, weasels, and snakes can squeeze through tiny holes. Raccoons can even figure out how to open simple latches!

NO CHICKEN WIRE!

This may sound funny, but never use chicken wire to build your coop or run. Chicken wire is designed to keep chickens in, not to keep predators out. Use ½-inch hardware cloth instead; it is stronger. Bury hardware cloth at least 12 to 18 inches deep all around the perimeter of the coop and run, or make a 3-foot-wide hardware cloth apron (a part that extends out) around the run.

Here are some other ways to protect your flock:

→ Use predator-proof locks on all windows and doors.

→ Automatic coop doors help to lock up the chickens in case you forget.

→ Hang solar-powered red blinking lights that mimic eyes from the coop and run them to deter predators at night.

→ Hang old CDs near the run — the reflection and movement deter birds of prey.

→ Regularly inspect your coop and run for breaches such as holes, or areas of deterioration where predators can squeeze through.

It's important to remove soiled shavings regularly, especially in a small coop like this one.

We like to sprinkle chicken-friendly fresh or dried herbs and flowers, such as mint, marigolds, and lavender, into each nesting box. Substances in these plants can help ward off poultry lice, mites, ticks, and flies.

A layer of straw in the run gives the hens something to scratch around in.

Cleaning the Coop

Keeping the coop clean and dry contributes to a healthy flock. Some people clean weekly, while others use a deep litter method. The deep litter method continually adds new bedding to the existing dirty bedding, which cuts down on frequent coop cleaning. You still have to clean the entire coop a few times per year and start over again. In the winter, this method helps generate heat in the coop.

We prefer to clean our small coop more frequently. Each week we scoop out the soiled pine shavings from the nesting boxes and coop floor and either add them to the compost pile or toss them into the run. Next, we wipe down the linoleum floor and the roosts with distilled white vinegar or a commercial coop cleaner.

Once that dries, we sprinkle the coop floor and nesting boxes with food-grade diatomaceous earth. (**Warning**: Diatomaceous earth can cause lung disease if breathed in over a period of many years. When distributing it, make sure the coop is well ventilated. Wearing a mask is an option.) Last, we add a fresh layer of kiln-dried pine shavings.

CLEANING THE RUN

Cleaning the run is important to prevent odors and flies, and it's even easier than tidying the chicken coop. The main thing is to clear away the poop, which you can do daily, or as needed. Don't allow puddles to form in the run, as standing water can promote disease. If the run does begin to smell, try a light dusting of Sweet PDZ, a natural odor absorber.

ESTABLISHING A FREE-RANGING FLOCK

Free-ranging is when you allow your chickens to wander wherever they like.

Free-ranging gives your birds plenty of exercise while they're eating bugs, worms, and grasses. As they scratch around, they till the soil and add fertilizer. However, if you have a free-ranging flock, you must be willing to risk losing one or two birds, or even the entire flock, to predators.

Some people accept this risk and let their birds out all day long, counting them at night when they come in to roost. Others allow their flocks out of the run only when they are home to watch them. By babysitting your flock, you can prevent them from getting into trouble from, say, eating poisonous mushrooms. You can keep the family dog away from them. You can shoo them away from off-limits places, such as the vegetable garden.

Free-ranging chickens are great in many ways, but they can make a big mess of the yard! (See chapter 10 for more about having chickens in the garden.)

We like to let our birds out in the early evening, around dusk. First, this means you don't have to chase after them to round them up, because they will naturally return to the coop as night falls. Second, it's a time when daytime predators are settling down for the night, but nighttime predators are just waking up.

PROS

→ Allows more space and exercise for the flock

→ Allows you to have a smaller coop and run

→ Provides supplemental food source; decreases the amount of chicken feed needed

→ Provides access to grasses, which are good sources of vitamins and omega-3 fatty acids

→ Helps prevent boredom and the development of bad habits such as feather picking

→ Allows hens to eat bugs, ticks, slugs, and other yard pests

→ Fertilizes your garden beds

→ Entertains family and friends

CONS

→ Increases risk of injury and predation

→ Neighbors might object if chickens wander into their yards

→ Flock might damage plants and crops

→ Increases chicken poop in the yard

→ Some hens may hide a nest of eggs

→ The flock is more likely to roost in trees instead of returning to the coop in the evening

6 FEEDING YOUR FLOCK

Chickens require age-appropriate food, fresh drinking water, and grit to help with digestion.

As your chickens rapidly grow from day-old chicks into full-size chickens, they will require a variety of chicken feed. Hens older than 20 weeks of age require a calcium source to help them build strong eggshells when they begin laying. And chickens of all ages need grit to make their digestive systems work properly.

It's Not Just Chicken Feed

From birth to six weeks of age, chicks require a feed formulation known as chick feed. This feed is finely ground for new babies. At around six weeks of age, your chicks will transition to a grower feed. They will remain on this feed until they are approximately 20 weeks of age. After that, the entire flock should be on layer feed that contains at least 16 percent protein. If you decide to keep a rooster or two, they can eat the same diet as the pullets and hens.

Chick feed comes in medicated and non-medicated versions. It isn't necessary to use medicated chick feed, but it does help to prevent a serious illness called coccidiosis. If you have your chicks vaccinated against coccidiosis (see page 74), then you should feed them non-medicated feed.

Chicken feed comes in a variety of formulations including mash, crumbles, and pellets. The nutritional value is the same in all three, with usually little to no difference in cost. Some people find that their chickens have a preference. I think that our chickens waste much less food when we use the pellets. Some feel that crumbles or mash are easier to use than pellets if you add supplements or medication.

Transition your six-week-old chicks to the grower feed slowly. At first, they may hesitate to eat something new, just like some kids! If you are using pellets, mix a few in with the chick feed. Over the course of a couple of weeks, you can increase the amount of whole pellets until your chickens are eating only the regular-sized pellets.

If you find that the chicks aren't eating the whole pellets (sometimes bantams take a while to adjust), have an adult help you crush a few whole pellets into smaller bits, then mix those in with the chick feed and a few whole pellets. Both standard chickens and bantam-sized chickens can eat pellets without any difficulty.

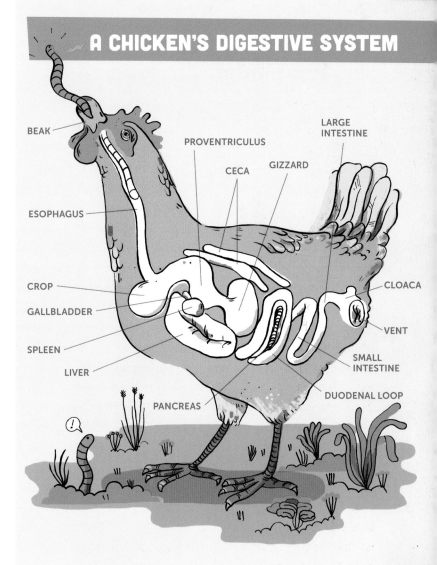

A CHICKEN'S DIGESTIVE SYSTEM

BEAK

PROVENTRICULUS

LARGE INTESTINE

CECA

GIZZARD

ESOPHAGUS

CLOACA

CROP

GALLBLADDER

VENT

SPLEEN

SMALL INTESTINE

LIVER

DUODENAL LOOP

PANCREAS

pellets

chick feed

CALCIUM

Calcium is essential to the egg-laying process as it makes the eggshells strong and thick. This prevents the eggs from breaking and also helps to curtail egg abnormalities. Chicks under 20 weeks should not be offered calcium, as it can interfere with proper bone development.

Layer chicken feed does contain calcium; however, the amount is usually not enough. So it's a good idea to provide a dish of calcium separately from the feed and the grit. The hens will ingest the calcium when their bodies require it. Calcium is readily available at feed stores in the form of crushed oyster shells.

You can also feed the chickens' eggshells back to them. It's free and fun to recycle eggshells in this manner, and it's also very simple.

As you use your eggs, rinse out the eggshells and set them aside to dry. When you have a pile of eggshells, place them on a baking sheet and bake at 200°F (93°C) for one hour. This kills off any lingering bacteria such as salmonella.

Remove them from the oven and allow them to cool. Transfer the shells to a sheet of newspaper and crush them into small pieces with a rolling pin.

GRIT

To digest their food properly, chickens need access to grit, which is coarse sand or tiny gravel that helps to grind up food in their digestive tract.

Grit comes in two sizes: chick-sized grit and grit for older birds. Be sure to provide the proper size grit for the age of your flock.

Provide the grit in a small dish separate from their feed. This way your birds can decide when they need grit. If you free-range your chickens and they have access to dirt, they will naturally ingest grit from the soil as they explore.

Crush the shells into tiny pieces so your hens don't recognize them as eggs. You don't want them to start eating freshly laid eggs, which is a hard habit to break once it starts.

chick grit

crushed oyster shells

crushed eggshells

grit for older birds

DIETARY SUPPLEMENTS

We like to incorporate traditional and natural techniques in keeping our flock healthy and thriving. These products are not mandatory, but I believe the ones discussed here can make a difference.

Nonetheless, the bottom line is that if one of your chickens is ill or has a bad infestation of worms, natural treatments alone might not be effective. When in doubt, seek proper medical treatment for your ill bird, including a visit to an avian vet, isolation from the flock, and proper medication. See chapter 8 for more about chicken health care.

Apple cider vinegar, the raw variety.

The kind with the "mother" — a natural by-product of the fermentation process — is packed with valuable vitamins and nutrients. It promotes digestive health and acidifies the digestive tract to help prevent harmful bacteria and fungi, such as yeast, from growing.

Try adding 1 tablespoon per gallon of water, but use it only in plastic waterers. Metal waterers will eventually rust. We add vinegar to only one of our two waterers. Look for raw apple cider vinegar with the "mother" at health food stores.

Diatomaceous earth (DE), food grade.

This fine powder is made of millions of microscopic fossils with very sharp edges. It is chock-full of minerals. In our experience, it helps keep bugs or insects out of the feed. Some people also believe that it acts as a natural dewormer for the flock.

Try adding 2 percent (by volume) of food-grade DE to your chickens' feed (for example, for every 3 cups of chicken feed, add approximately 1 tablespoon of DE).

Garlic.

Adding garlic to your chickens' diet can help to keep coop odor down, keep biting insects away, decrease cholesterol in eggs, and act as a natural dewormer. Surprisingly, it doesn't affect the flavor of the eggs.

You can sprinkle garlic powder on your flock's feed at a rate of up to 3 percent of the total volume (for example, for every 3 cups of chicken feed, add approximately 1½ tablespoons of garlic powder). You can also add a few cloves of crushed fresh garlic to their drinking water.

Pumpkin seeds.

In addition to providing vitamins, some evidence suggests that pumpkin seeds can decrease the worm population in your flock. Cucurbitacin is the active ingredient; it is also found in cucumber seeds and squash seeds.

Vitamins and electrolytes.

Vitamins and electrolytes can be very helpful during times of stress, such as shipping, heat stress, molting, severe temperatures, injury, and illness. You can add either a powder or a dissolvable tablet to your flock's drinking water. We usually add vitamins and electrolytes to one of our waterers at least once per week (not the one with the apple cider vinegar).

Yogurt.

Plain unflavored yogurt is a treat that your flock will enjoy. It is full of calcium and probiotics for better digestion. Researchers at the University of Florida have found that giving chickens milk also curtails egg eating. We feed our flock approximately 1 cup per six hens per week, in an old ceramic bowl.

Water Is Vital

Chickens must have access to fresh clean water at all times. Chicks need special waterers at first. Once the flock gets a bit older, you will find a variety of sizes from one gallon to many gallons. Calculate the size of your waterer based on the size of your flock and how much space you have in the coop.

If you have more than four chickens, you may want to offer water in a second spot. I like to keep two waterers for my flock, one in the coop and one outside in the run. With a flock of eight birds, we typically refill our two-gallon waterers twice per week, although that varies depending on the weather. Chickens drink more water during warmer days.

Keep the waterers clean and full. Scrub them out at least once per week with a little bit of distilled white vinegar and a plastic scrub brush that you use only for that job.

Many types of waterers are available, made in both plastic and metal. There are hanging styles and ones that sit on the ground, and even heated ones, which can be handy for long cold winters.

This waterer is made from a five-gallon beverage dispenser fitted with a nipple dispenser and set on some blocks. This system keeps the water clean and off the ground.

WHY I LOVE CHICKENS!

HADDIE, Age 12, East Haddam, Connecticut

How long have you been keeping chickens?
I started showing chickens with 4-H about three years ago, but we've had guinea fowl for over ten. We got started with chickens by chicken-sitting one summer for a friend. The four girls ended up staying permanently!

What do you love about keeping chickens?
I love keeping chickens because they are so very sweet and entertaining.

Do you have a favorite breed and why?
I don't really have a favorite breed. I think they all have unique personalities and traits; however I am very fond of the Speckled Sussex breed. With their beautiful speckled feathers and friendly personalities, they are a joy to have.

What is your favorite thing about chickens?
I enjoy showing my poultry and answering questions about poultry in general. People seem to enjoy meeting my birds and learning more about them! I also enjoy sitting with my flock and reading a book or sharing a snack with them. (They eat my food, but I don't eat theirs!)

Do you have any advice for other kids just getting started?
I would recommend researching as much as possible *before* bringing home chicks or chickens.

Feeding Treats

Chickens need to get most of their nutrition from chicken feed, but don't we all love a treat now and then? Well, so do chickens! You can feed them kitchen scraps or buy them special treats such as meal worms, black sunflower seeds, or scratch. Scratch is a mix of cracked, whole, and rolled grains; a handful of it can keep your flock happily entertained pecking and, of course, scratching, but it doesn't offer complete nutrition.

Too many treats can affect the quality and quantity of egg production as well as the flock's overall health.

Fresh fruit is a treat that chickens always enjoy.

GOOD TREATS, BAD TREATS

Chickens are curious and will taste just about anything they think might be edible. They love kitchen scraps, and you can offer them almost anything that you eat yourself.

This includes dairy products (hard cheeses, milk, plain unsweetened yogurt, and cottage cheese); cereal, grains, and bread (unsweetened, whole grain); and most fruits and vegetables.

But some foods aren't good for them. **Don't** feed your flock any of the following:

- ⊘ Caffeine or alcohol

- ⊘ Overly salty or sugary foods

- ⊘ Avocado

- ⊘ Citrus

- ⊘ Uncooked legumes, beans, and peas

- ⊘ Onions

- ⊘ Raw potatoes, or potato peels or foliage

- ⊘ Rhubarb

- ⊘ Tomato leaves

- ⊘ Uncooked rice

GROW MEALWORMS

Chickens love this protein-rich treat, but it can be expensive to buy them. You can purchase mealworm beetles from your local feed store or online. If you find live mealworms at a pet-supply store, you can also let them grow into beetles to start the whole cycle. They can be kind of stinky, so keep them in the basement or outside, weather permitting.

This is just one of many ways to raise mealworms. Learn more online and see what technique works best for you.

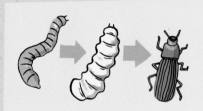

Mealworms are actually the larvae of the mealworm beetle. The beetles lay hundreds of eggs and then die. After the worms hatch, they develop to the pupa stage before becoming adults.

WHAT YOU NEED

- Plastic or glass container with lid, at least 9 inches in diameter
- Small piece of fine screen
- Scissors
- Duct tape
- A few cups of chicken feed or bran flakes, or a combination
- Half an apple, unpeeled
- Brown paper bag
- Mealworm beetles

Bonus: Almost everything in your mealworm habitat is edible for the flock!

What You Do

1. Cut a small hole in the lid and tape the screen to the underside. Put a few inches of feed in the container. Push the apple, cut-side up, into the feed.

2. Cut a circle of paper the same diameter as the container and place it over the feed. Add the beetles. They will hide under the paper.

3. Check on your beetles frequently, replenish the food as necessary, and replace the apple when it begins to mold.

Mealworms that are golden brown in color are ready for harvesting. You can pick them out of the habitat one by one, or you can just scoop out a handful and toss them into the run with the chickens.

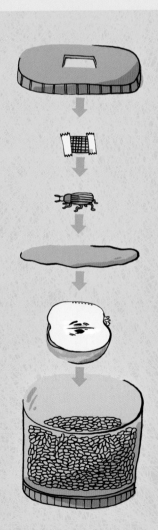

7 THE EXCITEMENT OF EGGS

You have taken good care of your flock, and the hens are finally old enough to start laying eggs. You've noticed that their wattles and combs have become a deeper, richer shade of red as they mature. Some of them may even be sitting in empty nesting boxes, as if practicing for the big day.

If it seems as though it is taking forever for your chickens to lay their first eggs, you are not alone. I still remember discovering our first egg.

It was a fall afternoon, and I was the only one home. I was raking leaves when I heard a commotion. All of the chickens were out in the run and one of the Silkies was yelling loudly. They all seemed fine, so I checked the nesting boxes. When I lifted the lid, the entire flock hurried inside the coop — they were curious, too! There in the box was a tiny, sweet, warm egg.

Over the next several weeks, all of the girls started laying. The kids raced out to the coop after school to check for eggs and suddenly we had dozens of them in our fridge.

When to Expect the First Eggs

Bantam breeds typically start to lay eggs around 20 weeks of age, while the larger standard-sized hens, like Buff Orpingtons, begin closer to 24 weeks. Once a hen begins to lay eggs, she produces one approximately every 26 hours. This is how long it takes for an egg to form.

Some days every hen will lay an egg, but on other days, you might discover only one egg from the whole flock. Egg production depends on their nutrition, their health, their age, and the seasons. Chickens lay eggs their entire lives but are the most productive during the first two years of life. This is not always the rule, but it is true in most cases.

Each hen lays eggs that are unique to her. Of course the color is consistent for the breed, but the eggs will typically have a shape and tint that is recognizable. If you have only a few hens, catching them in the act of laying and figuring out which egg belongs to which chicken should be pretty easy. Make sure that all the hens in your flock are regularly laying eggs, as this is a very good indicator of their health. Stress-free, healthy, young chickens lay eggs regularly.

QUICK CHICK FACTS

→ When the pullets' combs and wattles begin to turn a deeper shade of red, they are close to laying their first eggs.

→ You can usually tell what color eggs a hen will lay by the color of her earlobes. White lobes often mean white eggs and red lobes mean brown eggs!

Can you guess which chicken laid which egg?

Oyster Cracker

Feathers

Tilly

Dolly

Sunshine

Key: 1) Oyster Cracker, 2) Feathers, 3) Dolly, 4) Sunshine, 5) Tilly

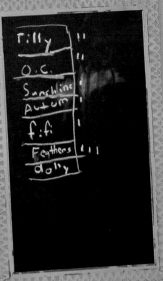

RECORD KEEPING

We hung a small chalkboard in our coop to make it easy to keep track of egg production. It's fun to know which hens have laid an egg each day. It's also a good way to notice if one of them stops laying.

EGG EATING

Chickens may begin to eat eggs for a number of reasons. These include boredom, curiosity, or lack of protein. Once egg eating starts, it is very difficult to correct.

You can try to prevent it by harvesting eggs frequently, ensuring the hens are on a good layer feed, and providing them with oyster shells.

You can also switch to slanted nesting boxes, where the egg rolls into a compartment that the hens can't reach. Or try filling a blown-out egg with mustard and leaving it as bait in the nesting box.

Before you assume that your hens are eating eggs, make sure that another sort of critter, like a snake, is not sneaking into the coop. Some predators leave the hens alone and go for the eggs.

How to Collect Eggs

Harvest your eggs from the nesting boxes three times per day, if possible: in the morning, the afternoon, and right before closing them in at night. Keeping the nest boxes empty curtails broody behavior and prevents chickens from developing the bad habit of egg eating.

Carefully collect all eggs from the nesting boxes, using a small bowl or an egg-collecting basket to hold them. If a hen is in the box, you can gently reach underneath her from the front and see if she is sitting on any eggs — sometimes one box becomes a favorite with all the hens. Use caution, as you do not want to startle her, especially if she is laying an egg herself.

If you find a broken egg or if you break an egg, remove all the soiled litter and egg from the nesting box. You do not want chickens to discover how delicious their eggs can taste! Eating eggs doesn't hurt the chickens, but it is distressing to watch, not to mention that you want all those eggs yourself!

If you have a rooster, it is especially important to collect eggs regularly on hot days, as fertilized eggs can start to develop at 85°F (29.4°C). Sometimes free-ranging hens will hide a nest of eggs away from the nesting boxes. If you find eggs outside the coop, you won't know how old they are. To be safe, it's best to discard them. The chickens will lay more.

Collecting eggs is a fun chore. You never know how many you'll find!

How to Clean Eggs

If you keep your nesting boxes clean and do not let your chickens sleep in them, then your hens' eggs should remain clean. If your nesting boxes are dirty, your eggs will be dirty. Develop the habit of tidying up the nesting boxes each morning when you open the coop up for the flock. A kitty litter scooper works wonderfully for scooping up chicken poop that is sometimes left in the nesting boxes.

One of the most important reasons to keep the nesting boxes clean is because you truly do not want to have to wash your eggs. Right before the hen lays an egg, she coats the entire shell with something called the bloom. The bloom keeps the egg fresh and helps prevent moisture, bacteria, fungi, and viruses from entering through the tiny pores in the eggshell. If you are harvesting eggs immediately after they have been laid, you might find an egg that is still wet. That's the bloom! Give it a minute or two to dry before handling it.

If you come across a badly soiled egg, you can clean it, but because you will wash off the bloom, you should store that egg in the fridge and eat it sooner than ones with the bloom still intact.

To clean an egg, turn on the faucet and adjust the temperature of the water to about 10 degrees warmer than the egg. Wash the egg gently under the flowing water until it is clean, then immediately dry it off. Don't submerge the egg in a bowl of water, which can promote bacteria passing through the shell. You don't need to use anything but water to clean your eggs, although commercial egg wipes are available.

How to Store Eggs

As long as the eggs have not been washed and the bloom is still intact, you can keep them on the counter until they are ready for use or until space is available in the refrigerator. They can stay at room temperature for up to a week. Fertilized eggs, however, should be refrigerated, especially in warm weather.

You can, of course, refrigerate eggs if you prefer, and this is the law if you wish to sell them. Once eggs have been refrigerated, they must stay refrigerated — you can't take them out of the refrigerator later and store them at room temperature.

Eggs are usually quite clean if you collect them right away, but sometimes you have to wash dirt or poop off one or two.

SELLING YOUR EGGS

At some point, your neighbors and friends will probably ask if you sell your eggs. And you most certainly will have extra eggs if you are a family of four and keep more than six hens. The number of eggs will fluctuate as the seasons change, but it's fun to load up a wagon with a cooler full of extras to sell to the neighbors (with your parents' permission, of course).

You can also set up a little farm stand with a cooler and a cash box at the end of your driveway that works on the honor system. Just check with your town first to see if it has regulations regarding farm stands or any other rules about selling eggs.

Store eggs between 33° and 45°F (1°–7°C) in the interior of the fridge as opposed to on the door, where the temperature fluctuates too much. You can use egg cartons, but a kitchen bowl works nicely, too. Also, do not keep eggs near stinky foods, such as cut onions. They can absorb odors through their porous shells, which could affect their taste.

Reasons for a Decline in Eggs

Many factors can affect the number of eggs that you collect each day. Sometimes you have to be a detective to determine the cause. As mentioned earlier, the number of eggs will decrease as your flock ages, but if that's not the reason, here are some questions to ask:

→ Has the weather been excessively hot or cold?

→ Is your flock feeling stressed out by predators?

→ Have your hens been eating too many treats?

→ Are they getting enough calcium?

→ Have they developed the bad habit of eating their own eggs?

→ Are your chickens molting?

→ Is an egg-eating predator to blame?

MOLTING

After your chickens are a year old, they will molt annually. Molting is the process that allows your chickens to replace their feathers. Usually it happens in the fall to replace old and worn-out feathers for the upcoming winter. However, chickens may spontaneously molt when they are stressed. Starting at the head, then the chest, wings, back, breast, and tail, the feathers begin to fall out. Sometimes my kids laugh when they see the chickens molt. One day the chickens look fine, the next day, feathers are everywhere. It looks like a chicken exploded in the coop!

Molting requires a great deal of protein. Since both feathers and eggs are made up almost entirely of protein, do not be surprised if your chickens stop laying eggs until their molt is complete, which can take up to a month.

During their molts, treat your hens to some high-protein snacks such as mealworms and sunflower seeds. You can also add some vitamins and electrolytes to their drinking water. Their main food source should continue to be their normal layer feed.

It will take about a month for this molting hen to completely regrow her feathers.

Chicken Trail Mix

Making snacks for chickens is great fun! You can create so many fabulous combinations. Mix up a few of your concoctions from the suggested ingredients list below and make up names for your recipes. Keep notes on which ones are your flock's favorites.

INGREDIENTS
Sunflower seeds
Cracked corn
Raisins
Peanuts
Oats
Assorted dried seeds such as
    millet, flax, pumpkin
Dried peas, carrots, broccoli,
    strawberries, blueberries
Dried crickets and mealworms

Mix up your chosen ingredients in a large lidded container. Treat your chickens to a handful of chicken trail mix as you like. Store it covered in a cool, dry place.

Issues with Eggs

Every so often, a malfunction occurs in a hen's egg-laying abilities. This can happen during any stage of her life. If you come upon a misshapen egg, just toss it away and monitor the next few eggs from that hen. Sometimes the problems are simply misfires, and other times they can indicate a more general health issue. If a health issue is the cause, you can intervene to help the hen return to normal egg laying.

EGGS WITHOUT SHELLS

You might think only rubber chickens lay rubber eggs, but eggs without shells are not uncommon when your hens first begin to lay, when they return to laying after molting, or as they age. Shell-less eggs are weird! They are soft and feel rubbery. The inner membrane of the egg is intact and what you pick up looks just like an egg except the shell is completely missing.

Eggs without shells are usually an indication that the hen is lacking calcium in her diet. To remedy this situation, be sure the flock has access to oyster shells or crushed eggshells. Also, be sure the flock is on a layer feed and that you are not feeding too many treats to your flock.

"WIND" EGGS

Sometimes hens will lay itty-bitty eggs, no larger than a quarter. These are called wind or fart eggs. Whichever name you prefer, these eggs are merely an "oops" in the hen's egg-laying process. These eggs are typically yolkless, and sometimes your hen will lay a few of these in a row. Eventually, your hen's egg laying should return to normal. You might find these eggs so cute that you want to blow them out to keep them! (See page 115 for directions.)

A BONUS: DOUBLE YOLKERS

Sometimes, you will crack open a large egg to reveal not one but two eggs inside! These double yolkers are quite a surprise and are completely edible. Consider yourself lucky to have a hen who occasionally makes these. They are a backyard chicken keeper's delight!

LET'S EGGS-PERIMENT!

Eggs are great for eating, but you can also do some cool experiments with them. Here are just three fun things to do with a few extra eggs.

Walking on Eggshells

Place two dozen eggs still in their cartons side by side and stand on top of them barefoot. What happens? Do they break? What do you think keeps them strong?

Egg Launchers

Can you drop an egg out of a second-storey window without breaking it? Give it a try!

Wrap a few eggs in padded containers using household items such as bubble wrap, toilet paper rolls, egg cartons, string, plastic bags, and a water bottle to keep them safe. You can even try making a parachute!

Then drop the eggs out a second-storey window. What happens? Which contraptions protect the eggs more?

Rubber Eggs

You can make a shell-less egg by placing a regular egg in a cup of white vinegar. Over the course of a few days, the vinegar will deplete the shell of calcium.

8 WHAT TO DO WITH A SICK CHICK

Kept in the right conditions, chickens are generally healthy, but even a well-cared-for bird can become sick or injured. Fortunately, you can do many things to prevent illness and injuries from happening with your flock. As Benjamin Franklin said, "An ounce of prevention is worth a pound of cure."

You can usually treat minor illnesses or injuries at home, but other times you might need to see a veterinarian who treats chickens. If you feel that one of your chickens might be sick, isolate her away from the flock until you have a proper diagnosis.

If your egg-laying hens require antibiotics, be sure to read the label and to discuss it with your veterinarian. Some medications cannot be used in egg-laying hens. Some medications also have a withdrawal period. This means that during and after administration of that medication, all eggs must be thrown away for a certain amount of time. Never give a chicken antibiotics or medication unless you know the exact diagnosis and what you are treating.

Keeping the Flock Healthy

One of the main things that you can do as a chicken keeper is to control the environment where your flock lives. Keeping a clean and neat living area helps your flock to remain healthy, as does feeding them good-quality feed and fresh water. Predator proofing is also important. (See chapter 5 for more on proper housing.)

It is important to check your flock every day. Sometimes this just means watching for a few minutes to be sure the chickens are acting normally. Make sure that each bird is lively, curious, moving about regularly, eating, drinking, and making well-formed poops.

When chickens are not feeling well, they will act sleepy, puff up their feathers, or stop interacting with others. They may cough or sneeze or have watery eyes. They may develop diarrhea. If very ill, they may not eat or drink.

A BASIC CHICKEN FIRST-AID KIT

You can treat many minor illnesses and injuries at home, so make a basic first-aid kit for your flock (see the list below). Keep it handy in a sealed plastic box near the coop. Include the phone number of a local veterinarian who treats chickens, along with a notepad and pen or pencil.

It's also a good idea to have a small pet carrier on hand to isolate any ill birds from the flock until they are diagnosed and while they are healing. A copy of *The Chicken Health Handbook* by Gail Damerow comes in handy, too.

→ Disposable latex gloves

→ 3% hydrogen peroxide (for superficial wound cleaning)

→ Blu-Kote (helps to curtail picking at a wound)

→ Neosporin (for superficial wound treatment)

→ Vetericyn (for more serious wounds)

→ VetRx (natural treatment for multiple ailments)

→ 1% hydrocortisone cream (for prolapsed vents)

→ Gauze and neoprene wrap

→ Nail clipper and nail file (for broken beaks or nails)

→ Tweezers

→ Scissors

→ Band-Aids or other brand of bandage (for broken toes or bent toes in chicks)

→ Superglue (for broken beaks)

→ Cornstarch (stops light bleeding from a nail or beak)

→ Vaseline (frostbite prevention for combs and wattles)

→ Old, clean towel (for wrapping an injured or ill chicken)

→ Flashlight

Keep a couple of hen saddles (material that fits over a hen's back and around her wings) on hand to protect wounds or prevent over-mating injuries.

HANDS-ON HEALTH CARE

It makes sense to accustom your chickens to being handled so you can get a good look at them if you need to. Peek under their wings and around their vents. Do you see any signs of pests? Are their eyes clear? Do you feel any swelling or wounds on their bodies? Inspect their feet, especially on the bottoms. Do you notice any lumps on the bottom of the foot? How are their toenails? How does their crop feel? These are the sorts of questions to ask as you use your eyes and hands to check out each of your flock members.

You don't need to handle each chicken on a daily basis, but if a chicken is showing signs of illness, you will need to act like a detective to figure out what is happening and how to help your chicken. Immediately separate any chicken who is acting ill from the rest of the flock. This is called quarantining. It keeps the sick chicken from infecting the others and allows her to recover in peace.

It's much easier to examine a hen that is used to being picked up than one that is struggling to escape!

WHY I LOVE CHICKENS!

XAVIER, Age 12, Williamstown, Massachusetts

How long have you been keeping chickens?
I have been keeping chickens for five years. In that time, we have had eight different breeds including an Ameraucana, a Dominique, and a Salmon Faverolle.

What do you love about keeping chickens?
I like that the chickens are our friends.

Do you have a favorite breed and why?
Ameraucana, because they are bearded and lay blue eggs.

What is your favorite thing about chickens?
I just like to hang out with them. I like to sit on the grass and let them walk around me and peck at my shoes. I can really observe them. Once I saw my chicken Leela stealing insects from a spider's web! I love watching my chickens doing funny things.

Do you have any advice for other kids just getting started?
Keeping chickens is fun, but you need to be responsible. Do not let them stay out after dark and don't let them go near the road. It's also helpful to know when predators such as foxes are learning to hunt, because juvenile animals tend to kill more. Two other animals to look out for are dogs and fisher cats. Do whatever you need to do to keep your flock safe.

Problems with Baby Chicks

Sometimes, despite your best efforts, bad things can happen to your birds. That is a normal part of keeping chickens. Problems can arise no matter what the age of the chicken. Even a tiny day-old chick can develop problems. Spend time watching your chicks and inspect them a couple times per day. For their size, they can wind up in a heap of trouble!

PASTY BUTT

Chicks poop a lot and sometimes dried poop builds up over their vents, a condition often called pasty butt. Other terms include sticky butt, pasting up, and pasting over. Silkie chicks seem to be especially prone to this condition, perhaps because of their fluff. Pasty butt can also develop from the use of poor-quality chick feed. If the situation is not remedied, the chick can die, so keeping an eye on the bottoms of your

Pasty butt can happen more than once to the same chick, but all chicks will outgrow it.

chicks is very important, even if it seems silly or gross.

Pasty butt is easy to treat. Gather a bowl of warm water, some paper towels, and a tube of triple antibiotic ointment. Carefully holding the chick, dip your thumb and pointer finger into the warm water and use them to gently moisten the poop. Keep dabbing it with water until it softens, then very gently work it off with your fingers. Do not just pull the poop off. You could cause severe injury.

Continue until the poop is completely removed. Dry the vent area with paper towels as best you can. Then apply a small dab of triple antibiotic ointment to the vent and return the chick to the brooder. Immediately wash your hands well with warm water and soap (or wear latex gloves, if you prefer).

COCCIDIOSIS

This serious illness is caused by coccidia, which are protozoa that thrive in moist, warm conditions, such as a dirty brooder. Chicks can easily become infected. They develop bloody diarrhea and can die quite quickly, so it's better to prevent this disease than to have to treat it.

The best thing you can do is keep your brooder clean and dry. You may have to clean up water spills and wet bedding a couple times each day. This is very important. Medicated chick feed that contains amprolium can help to prevent but not treat coccidiosis.

If any chicks develop bloody diarrhea, isolate them immediately and take a fecal sample to a vet to find out what drugs you need to treat that particular strain of the disease. There are also over-the-counter medicines for it.

VITAMIN AND ELECTROLYTE DEFICIENCY

Chicks grow so rapidly that they risk developing vitamin and electrolyte deficiencies. Symptoms include lack of energy, not eating or drinking, lying in the brooder with their legs extended, losing balance, falling down, or having a twisted or "wry" neck.

Poultry vitamins and electrolytes are readily available in most feed stores in tablet or powder form that you add to their drinking water. Be sure to read the package's directions. Add some vitamins to your chick's water source at least a couple times per week for the first few weeks, as a preventive.

FIXING FEET

Sometimes chicks develop problems with their feet or legs. It may look a bit scary at first, but the problem can often be easily corrected.

Curled Toes

You might notice that a chick's toes on one foot are curled and she is walking on the foot like a fist. This can happen from an injury during hatching or shortly after. When both feet have curled toes, it is usually from a lack of vitamins in the mother hen.

To correct curled toes, start by adding some vitamins and electrolytes to the brooder's water. Then gather a pair of scissors and a medium-sized adhesive bandage. Trim the sticky sides of the bandage to the same size as the gauze pad. Gently unfurl the chick's toes and place the foot on the gauze pad, with the toes sticking out slightly. Overlap the adhesive on top of the foot.

Return the chick to the brooder. Do not remove the bandage until it is almost falling off. The toes should straighten in about a week's time.

Splayed Leg Syndrome

Chicks' legs take a while to build up strength outside the shell. Until their muscles become strong, they are at risk for developing something called splayed leg syndrome. It can occur if the chicks live on slippery bedding, such as newspaper, for their first few days. It can also happen if the hen sits too hard on a chick.

A chick suffering from splayed leg may sit with one leg jutting out to the side or may appear as if she is doing a split. She cannot walk and will use her wings to move around.

Splayed legs can be corrected by hobble-splinting the legs above the "knees" so they remain close together. Over time, the chick will regain the muscle tone and strength to walk correctly. Hobble splints can be made from rubber bands, medical wraps, and medical tape. If you are having difficulty applying the splint, seek help from a veterinarian.

Here are some ways to keep
your chickens' crops healthy:

→ Provide grit at all times.

→ Avoid feeding large pieces
of foods that are hard
to digest such as corn
cobs or pieces of meat.

→ Add apple cider vinegar
to their drinking water
(1 tablespoon per gallon of
water) to keep yeast levels
balanced (see page 57).

→ Consider adding
probiotics to the flock's
food supply or water.

→ Don't feed sugary foods.

→ Keep your yard
clean of debris.

→ Keep grasses short
where chickens roam.

→ Remove straw and hay
from the coop and
run if your chickens
begin to eat it.

Common Chicken Problems

Grown chickens can also have a few health issues, such
as parasites or heat stress. It's important to keep an eye on
the crop, which is critical for digestion. Unfortunately, an
improperly functioning crop can develop one of several
problems, or even a combination of them.

IMPACTED CROP

The crop may stop functioning when it becomes clogged or
impacted. This can happen from an infection, or if the hen
eats long grasses (including hay and straw), tough foods,
or foreign objects. When the crop becomes impacted, the
chicken does not feel like eating and the crop remains full,
unable to empty.

A full normal crop feels about the size of a golf ball. An
impacted crop can grow to the size of a tennis ball and
can be tender and warm to the touch. If the crop becomes
impacted, you can try to move things along by isolating the
chicken and feeding her a diet of water and encouraging
her to eat soft bread soaked in olive oil. You can also try to
gently massage the crop to get things moving.

When treating an impacted crop, avoid regular feed and
don't give any extra treats. If the crop has not emptied or
your chicken's condition has not improved after a few days,
you might consider a trip to the veterinarian to have the
crop emptied.

SOUR CROP

When the delicate balance of the normal bacteria that live
in the chicken's digestive system becomes unbalanced,
yeast thrives. Chickens can develop yeast infections in their
crops. When this happens, their breath smells fruity and
their crops can feel gassy and bubbly. A crop can be sour
and impacted at the same time.

Sour crops can develop from an impacted crop, illness,
recent medication use, and worms. Unfortunately, sour
crop is not an easy thing to treat on your own. Some people
try home remedies, including probiotics, plain yogurt, or

adding apple cider vinegar to the water (see page 57). If these prove unsuccessful after a few days, you may need to ask your vet for an antifungal prescription medication to clear the infection.

PENDULOUS CROP

Pendulous crops occur when the muscles that hold the crop close to the chest become stretched and lose their strength. This can happen after a chicken has had an impacted crop or has been eating heavy foods. A chicken can thrive despite a pendulous crop, but be sure to pay a little extra attention to this chicken and check her crop regularly to be sure it is emptying and working properly.

When Tilly fills her crop with treats, it remains pendulous for a while, as you can see here.

FEATHER PICKING

Unfortunately, chickens sometimes peck at each other's feathers, even to the point of hurting each other. This behavior can stem from boredom, lack of protein in the diet, changes in the pecking order that lead to bullying, the presence of pests, or lack of space. Sometimes it's just one chicken who is doing this, but sometimes others begin to copy her and they may gang up on a particular hen. If that hen loses some feathers or bleeds a little from being pecked, the others will attack her even more.

Here are some ideas for preventing feather pecking:

→ Make sure your chickens aren't too crowded together.

→ Introduce boredom busters such as a cabbage piñata (page 85) or other long-lasting treat or add a shatterproof mirror to the coop.

→ Let the flock explore the yard, even just for a short time each day.

→ Give your chickens the correct feed for their age.

→ Do a hands-on inspection for pests such as poultry lice, mites, ticks, scaly leg mites, and fleas. Treat if necessary.

If none of the above work, consider finding another home for the problem chicken.

MITES, LICE, AND OTHER PESTS

Parasites are tiny creatures that live on another animal, usually by feeding on their blood. Some common parasites that thrive on chickens are mites, poultry lice, fleas, and ticks. The type of pests that might affect your flock will vary based on your location.

A severe pest infestation can cause chickens to become anemic, lose feathers, stop laying eggs, and even die. Prevention is essential, so become familiar with what these pests look like on chickens. Most pests tend to live around the vents of chickens.

Many products are available to treat a pest infestation, such as shampoos, dips, food-grade diatomaceous earth, herbal remedies, and natural sprays. To treat the problem effectively, know what type of parasite is bothering your flock. Even if you see parasites on only a few birds, you need to treat the whole flock and you should look at your coop management practices. Regularly cleaning and disinfecting the coop helps to prevent these pests from taking up residence and also breaks their life cycle if you do have an infestation.

I SPY SOME PESTS!

It's important to check your flock regularly for these common but very tiny pests.

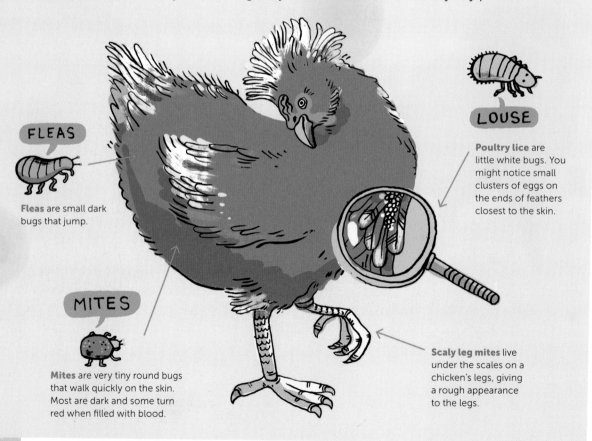

FLEAS

Fleas are small dark bugs that jump.

LOUSE

Poultry lice are little white bugs. You might notice small clusters of eggs on the ends of feathers closest to the skin.

MITES

Mites are very tiny round bugs that walk quickly on the skin. Most are dark and some turn red when filled with blood.

Scaly leg mites live under the scales on a chicken's legs, giving a rough appearance to the legs.

BOTANICAL BUG SPRAY FOR CHICKENS

WHAT YOU NEED

- 5 drops of lavender essential oil
- 10 drops of citronella essential oil
- 8 ounces of distilled water
- A small light-proof spray bottle, preferably aluminum

What You Do

1. Combine all of the ingredients in the spray bottle.

2. Shake well before applying to your dog or chickens.

Use this spray when your flock (and your dog!) are out and about wandering the yard and gardens.

My dog groomers turned me onto a homemade bug spray for dogs. They swore that if we sprayed our dog right before heading out for hikes in the woods, this spray would repel ticks and fleas. Well, it worked so beautifully, I decided to try it on the chickens! It seems to help them, too.

When spraying this on your chickens, be sure to avoid the head and eyes. Apply only to the back, chest, under the wings, and their fluffy bottoms. All of these ingredients and the spray bottle can most likely be found at your local natural food store.

PARASITIC WORMS

Common intestinal worms that live in chickens' digestive systems include roundworms, gapeworms, cecal worms, and hairworms. Worms can cause chickens to become anemic, lose weight, and have breathing difficulty. Although it happens very rarely, large roundworms can sometimes be found in an infested chicken's eggs!

Deworming chickens is a topic of some debate in the chicken-keeping community. Some people deworm their flocks regularly with medication, while others focus on preventive techniques.

Deworming with medication can be done every six months to a year. If you choose to deworm your flock, read the medication labels carefully. Some dewormers cannot be used in meat birds or in hens who are laying eggs. Often, an egg withdrawal time is required — during this time you need to throw away the eggs to be sure you do not ingest the wormer yourself.

Deworming a flock can be stressful on their bodies, so avoid deworming your flock when they are molting.

Non-medicated methods to try to prevent worms include adding food-grade diatomaceous earth or garlic powder to the feed, feeding the flock raw pumpkin seeds, and adding apple cider vinegar to the drinking water. (see page 57 for more details.)

EGG BOUND

Egg bound means that a hen is having difficulty passing a particularly large egg. Egg-bound hens typically sit in the nesting boxes, feathers poufed out, looking under the weather. You might notice her tail moving up and down. She might stop eating and drinking.

If you suspect that a hen is egg bound, gently take your hand and feel along the lower abdomen of the hen. It will feel full. Do not press too hard, as you do not want to break the egg inside. A broken egg inside the hen can lead to an infection called egg peritonitis.

If you suspect that you have an egg-bound hen, bring her inside and give her a good soak in the sink in warm (not hot) water with a little bit of Epsom salts added. Dry her with a towel and place her in a warm, quiet place. A dog carrier or a small animal cage, covered with a blanket, works perfectly.

Moist heat can help her to pass the egg, so you can try adding a heat lamp to the enclosure with a pan of warm water underneath the cage's wire floor to provide extra humidity. Just be careful she does not overheat.

If she does not pass the egg within 24 hours, you might need to take her to the vet for an injection that will stimulate her body to pass the egg.

VENT PROLAPSE

Sometimes if a hen has been passing rather large eggs or is recovering from being egg bound, her vent can turn a bit "inside out." If this happens you will notice soft, moist, pink tissue around the vent.

To treat this condition, apply a little 1% hydrocortisone cream to the vent twice a day until it improves.

HEAT STRESS

In the heat and humidity of summer, backyard chickens can easily become susceptible to heat stress. Heat stress is a potentially life-threatening condition in which a chicken is having difficulty cooling herself. Open-mouth panting, lifting the wings, and immobility are all signs of heat stress.

It is always best to prevent heat stress from happening in the first place. On the hottest of summer days, be sure your chickens have access to clean, cool drinking water. Be sure the coop is well ventilated; if it has a window, you might run a fan in it. You can evenoffer your flock an herbal wading pool (see page 82).

If a hen appears to be suffering from heat stress, remove her from the flock and place her in cool, not cold, water for a few minutes to try and bring her temperature down. It may take her a few days to recover. In the meantime, she should have access to plenty of water and shade.

When to Call the Vet

At certain times you will want to defer to the expertise and help of a veterinarian, preferably one who has been trained in avian health. So, when should you call a vet?

→ When you are unsure of why a chicken appears to be ill.

→ When you don't feel comfortable treating the problem.

→ When your chicken hasn't improved after 24 to 48 hours of home remedies.

→ When a major injury or predator attack could require surgery, stitches, or antibiotics.

→ When you think the chicken won't live and you want to give her a quick and painless end.

HOW TO FIND A VET

The Internet makes it easy to locate a nearby veterinarian. Vets who specialize in chickens can be difficult to locate. In a true emergency, I think you will find most vets would be willing to lend a hand with your ill chicken, but try to establish a relationship with a vet before a crisis.

With a grown-up's permission, search the Internet for vets in your area. Some words to use in your search include "avian veterinarian," "veterinarians who see chickens," or "locate a chicken vet." I also have a regularly updated list of chicken vets on my website, Tilly's Nest.

QUICK CHICK FACT

Chickens do not sweat. They rely on their combs and wattles for cooling.

HERBAL WADING POOL

In addition to making sure that your flock has plenty of shade and cool drinking water, you can provide them with this simple wading pool to make them more comfortable on especially warm days. If the weather is very hot, add some ice for an extra-cooling effect.

WHAT YOU NEED

- A disposable aluminum pan at least 3 inches high (I use a lasagna pan)
- Your flock's favorite fresh herbs and flowers, cut or torn into small pieces
- Water
- Ice (optional)

What You Do

1. Gather a few handfuls of herbs in the pan.

2. Place the pan in the run and fill it with cold water.

3. Add a few cups of ice.

The herbs will entice the chickens to explore the refreshing water. Some chickens will be content to pluck the herbs from the pan, while others may wade right in to cool their feet.

End of Life

Unfortunately, part of the circle of life involves saying goodbye to flock members when they pass away. Sometimes a chicken will fall ill and die, or you might lose one to a predator. Often, with pet chickens, they simply grow too old.

As hens age, their bodies change, just as humans do. You'll notice some of these changes as early as four years of age; others begin to show when the girls are around seven years old.

→ Combs and wattles shrink and become less smooth.

→ Legs and feet become thicker.

→ They lay fewer eggs on a less regular schedule.

→ They are less active.

→ They lose rank in the pecking order.

When you believe that your chicken is at the end of her life, you can bring her to your veterinarian for an injection that will quickly and painlessly put her to sleep. This humane service is something that most vets will do for any animal, even if they don't typically care for chickens.

When a chicken does pass away, bury her deep in the ground with an adult's help. These times can make you feel very sad, and that is normal and okay. Part of living with animals is accepting that they do not live as long as we do. Focus on the happy memories you have of this flock member.

CHICKEN SCHOOL

Saying Goodbye

Unfortunately, goodbyes are part of keeping chickens. Sometimes we must find new homes for flock members, and sometimes a beloved chicken passes away. Even a long life for a chicken seems too short to us. Saying goodbye is never easy, but beginnings and endings are part of life.

Chickens have their own way of adjusting to a loss and have helped my kids to understand the circle of life. An ill or very old chicken seems to know when her time has come. She may find a quiet place away from the flock. We witnessed each member of our flock visit with a dying chicken. Some chickens sat for a while, others clucked and cackled quietly. My kids said they were saying goodbye.

After a loss, the flock seems to remember the missing family member for a while, but they quickly establish a new pecking order and life goes on. When we are missing departed flock members, we go and share some treats with the girls. I like to think that somewhere from up among the clouds, those chickens are looking down at the coop, keeping watch over us.

9 HANDLING, TRAINING, AND PLAYING with Chickens

One of the most common questions I hear when I "chat chicken" with people is, "How do you get your chickens to be so friendly?" We do have a very friendly flock, for the most part. They enjoy a good petting. They love to sit in our laps and nuzzle into our necks, which I think of as chicken hugs.

The answer is that whether you are dealing with people or animals, it is very important to develop trust, and that takes time, effort, and patience.

Training chickens is much easier when you purchase them as baby chicks than if you buy chickens who are already a few weeks old. That doesn't mean you cannot train older birds, but it will take a bit longer and require a bit more time and dedication on your part.

People who have tame chickens know it's the result of showing their animals compassion, love, and good care. The respect and love will be mutual.

TREATS FOR YOUR FLOCK

Chicken Piñata

Chickens can get bored, especially during the winter, and bored chickens can get into all sorts of mischief, such as egg eating and feather picking.

To prevent these unwanted behaviors, offer your flock activities like this chicken piñata, to keep them occupied. It's lots of fun to watch the chickens peck, dodge, and run after the piñata.

SUPPLIES
One head of cabbage, broccoli, or cauliflower
One ball of garden twine
Scissors

1. Cut a piece of string about 6 feet long. Having one long piece of string is important so that none of the hens accidentally eats it.

2. Place the cabbage on the middle point of the string. Wrap the string completely around the widest portion of the cabbage and tie it together once.

3. Flip over the cabbage and thread the two loose pieces of string underneath the existing string. Tie them around the cabbage in the opposite direction.

4. You can tie the loose ends together to hang the cabbage on an existing hook or try looping the string through a support beam in the run. The finished piñata should be at the shoulder height of the chickens.

→ Chickens can carry
salmonella, a bacteria that
can make people very sick.

→ Don't touch your face or put
your hands in your mouth
while handling chickens.

→ You might be tempted
to kiss your chickens,
but don't do it! Gentle
hugs work just fine.

Handling New Chicks

As long as you handle baby chicks very gently, it is never too early to start. In fact, the first step is to hold your chicks frequently but without stressing them. Whether you are dealing with baby chicks or older chickens, hold them properly, as shown in the pictures here. This is for their safety and yours, as well as their comfort. When you are dealing with baby chicks, you should be aware that their bones are very delicate. Hold them firmly but gently, being careful not to squeeze them too tightly or you might injure them.

All chicks will be skittish of you at first. This behavior is part of their natural instinct to keep safe. Can you blame them? What would you think if you were tiny and a giant was trying to grab you?

HOW TO TAME A CHICK

Start taming your chicks with the way you approach the brooder. Come up to it slowly and quietly. Don't make sudden movements with your hands as you refill the food and water dishes. Let your hand rest quietly in the brooder. You will find that the curious chicks will eventually come to investigate. Over time, the chicks learn not to fear your hands, which will become very important in the future. When you are reaching into the nesting boxes, sometimes under hens, to gather eggs, you want them to be friendly and to stay calm.

Once your new chicks are active and eating well, you can begin to handle them. Slowly reach out and grasp one gently in your hand, approaching from behind and putting your hand over her wings. Once you have the chick, place your other hand under her feet to make a sort of cup where she'll feel warm and safe. Keep your hands over her wings so she can't flap them.

Next, sit down on the ground and hold the chick in your lap, keeping your hands cupped gently around her. Sitting is very important for the chick's safety — if you were to accidentally drop the chick or she were to jump from your hands, she won't fall as far.

Always thoroughly wash your hands before and after handling chicks. Also immediately remove any pooped-on clothing and put it in the laundry.

As you feel the chick begin to relax, place her on your leg. Still keeping one hand lightly over the wings, gently stroke the chick with the finger of your other hand. Stroke the chick's back, neck, and head. The chick might even let out a pleasure trill. It sounds like the purring of a cat, only cuter!

As the chick becomes more comfortable, she may fall asleep on you. When you are done holding your chick, gently return her to the brooder and pick up the next chick.

TAKE IT SLOWLY

At first, you may be able to hold each chick for only a couple of minutes before she begins to wiggle. They are skittish and need time to adjust to being held. Try to extend the time you hold them to a few minutes each day. Be sure you hold all of your chicks rather than just the same one each time. You will surely have your favorites, but if you want the entire flock to feel comfortable around people, you must handle them all. If other family members would like the chickens to bond with them, encourage them to spend time holding the chicks, too.

After holding the chicks daily for a couple of weeks, your hard work will begin to pay off and you will begin to notice some behavioral changes. When you visit the brooder, they will pay attention to you and say "hello." They will approach you. You will not have to chase them, because they will enjoy your company. It is a very rewarding feeling!

When your chicks are about four weeks old, you can introduce them to a treat. This is something special that you can use to train them to return to you when they are free-ranging or have escaped. A special treat is also helpful when you need to examine

We have a two-finger rule in our house, and it is a good rule to keep. We ask everyone who wants to pet the animals to do so with only their pointer and middle fingers held together.

a member of the flock. At our place, these treats are usually dried mealworms or raisins. As you share these treats, use a "call" word with it. Introduce the treat by using your call word, then give the treat. Do this every time you give this special treat. The chickens will learn to associate your call word with treats and will soon come running. Our call word is a long, singsongy *Gur-rrr-llls*.

Finally, even as your flock transitions from the brooder to the outside coop, you should continue to spend quality time with them. Teach them, treat them, and handle them as frequently as you can. Don't be surprised if they call to you, follow you, and spend time with you in the yard. Our flock always wants to know what we're doing. They watch as the kids dig holes for new plantings. As I pull weeds, they scratch in the discarded pile. And they love to investigate what's new in the compost pile!

Holding a Hen

Most of the same principles apply when handling full-grown birds. If your chickens are already tame, then you should have little to no difficulty holding them. Just remember that chickens are a lot heavier and stronger than chicks. Be sure to use both hands to pin their wings to their bodies so they can't flap. Flapping wings is an escape technique, and it naturally happens when a chicken is nervous or scared.

Reaching from above, place your cupped hands on each side of the hen and hold her wings to her body. Lift her up and hold her close to your body near your lower chest. Chickens have a natural instinct to peck, so keep her face away from yours, especially away from eye level. It is not necessary to put your hand under her feet. In fact, doing that provides her with leverage to escape.

Try cradling the chicken on your hip. Hold one wing against your side and wrap your arm and hand over the other side of the chicken. Some folks face the chickens backward when holding them this way, with their fluffy butts facing forward. This is the best way to avoid being pooped on!

LAP TIME!

Once your chickens are comfortable being carried and held while you stand, you can sit down and hold them. They will usually stay put and not flap their wings. Eventually, they will appreciate you gently scratching areas that are hard for them to reach, like the back of the head. They will wriggle into your fingertips and close their eyes happily.

As you spend time with your flock, you will realize that some chickens are just more lovable than others. Some want to spend all their time with you, while others are content to scratch around and just be in your company. They still love you, but they don't crave a human touch. That is normal and okay.

Our largest chicken, Oyster Cracker, is our lap chicken. She loves attention. After I am done holding her, chatting with her, and petting her, I return her to the ground. As soon as I put her down, she hops up and wants more. Sometimes she does this four or five times!

Gently pin the wings down with your hands before picking up a chicken. A flapping bird is hard to hold onto!

Taming Adult Hens

Training an older bird is more difficult but can be done. Start by putting a low seat, such as a milk crate, in the run and spending some time sitting there. The flock needs to become accustomed to your presence at times other than when you are doing coop maintenance.

Pick a time of day, such as late afternoon, when the flock is calming down for the day. Do not try first thing in the morning, as they are bursting with energy then. Put the family dog out of sight, inside the house. Keep a quiet environment, meaning no loud music, no other kids running around, or anything else that might distract or startle your flock.

Here are some basic guidelines:

→ Sit still and just watch.

→ Don't engage the flock unless they come to you.

→ Don't try to hold them at first.

→ Talk to them so they get used to your voice.

→ Have treats ready (raisins or grapes cut in half are good).

Once the chickens begin to come closer, talk to them and toss a couple of treats on the ground. This action will immediately identify you as a treat giver. Once they are comfortable hanging out near your feet, try placing a couple of treats in your hand and see if the chickens will take the treats from your palm. Be very still.

As the chickens grab the treat from your hand, they will peck you a little. Feeling that peck might surprise you at first, but it doesn't hurt, so try to stay still and not jerk your hand away. Jumping or pulling back could undo all of your hard work. After a few days, the flock will begin to realize what your visits are all about. They will "dance" at the front of the coop door, eager to see you.

Once the flock is comfortable eating out of your hand, see if they will let you stroke the feathers on their backs. Let them get used to this. Soon enough, one or two chickens will jump into your lap for treats. When they do that, pet them and soothe them with encouraging words. They might even sit for a spell.

When your flock reaches this comfort level, you can try picking up one of the friendlier birds. At first, try holding her while you are standing up, so she can't push against your lap to escape. Hold her for only a few seconds at first, then reward her with a treat.

This process can take weeks to months to accomplish. Many factors will affect how quickly your flock becomes comfortable with you. For example, the frequency of your visits, the breeds you have selected, and your dedication to the process all play a big part.

Teaching your flock to eat from your hand is a great way to start their training.

Speaking Chicken

Chickens use nearly 30 recognizable phrases to communicate within the flock, from tiny little guttural rumblings in the back of the throat to full-out squawking. If you spend enough time with the flock, you can learn what they are saying.

People often say that in order to learn a language that you don't know, you should move to a place where that language is primarily spoken. Lucky for you, learning chicken chat just means spending more time around the flock. You will pick up a few phrases before you know it!

One morning, I realized that I was mixing English with little strings of chicken sounds, such as *buh-dup*. This phrase starts as a low sound and rolls up, like a question. The chickens use it to say *Hello* or *What are you up to?*

Another one is a low *doh, doh, doh*, deliberate and repetitive. I call these whispering sounds "comfort calls." Mother hens use them to communicate with their babies. The flock uses them as they settle onto their roosts, and we mimic them as we tuck them in for the night.

Tilly, our most talkative hen, always has much to say. Now that I've spent a lot of time listening, watching, and paying attention, Tilly and I can have a makeshift conversation.

Dealing with Bullies

One spring day, I stopped by the feed store for some chicken feed and fell in love with a tiny Silver Laced Wyandotte chick. I took her home and named her Dottie Speckles. She was adorable, but, unfortunately, as she grew, she began to terrorize the other hens, especially the Silkies. She would pull puffs of feathers off their heads, leaving peck marks. The other chickens avoided her. No one ate with her. The entire flock seemed uncomfortable, and they began laying fewer eggs.

At first, I thought that Dottie Speckles was just climbing up the pecking order. But after she became the head hen, her behavior only worsened. I finally had to admit that she was just not a nice hen. She had become a bully.

Even though she liked people and would let us hold her, we knew that Dottie Speckles needed to go to a new home. Fortunately, a friend who keeps many chickens was willing to take her. It was the right decision. With Dottie Speckles gone, the entire flock relaxed, and the eggs became abundant again.

Dottie didn't change, though. She was paired up with a rooster, and one night she removed every feather from his head! In 40 years of keeping chickens, the farmer had never met a chicken who behaved like that. Dottie was fortunate to find a new solo life as a pet.

The world will never be free from bullies. Unfortunately, they are a part of life. But it helps if we try to understand them. Sometimes bullies have trouble at home. They don't feel good about themselves, so they pick on other people. Some of them are lonely and don't know how to make or treat friends. Some are copying their parents being mean to other adults.

Even though Dottie Speckles seemed to be born with a mean streak, I don't think people start out as bullies. I believe they learn to act that way. Still, bullying is not acceptable and it is not cool. Try to avoid bullies when you can. One day they will learn that life will be pretty lonely if they continue to bully other people.

The kids and I use chicken chat as much as possible. We call to them to return to the coop after free-ranging, or when we need to catch them in a hurry. When our girls meet new people, they are sometimes a bit skittish until I quietly cluck to them that they are safe. Immediately, they let down their guard and begin to welcome their new friends.

Sometimes, I give a low rolling growl while flicking my tongue on the roof of my mouth. When they hear that warning call, they freeze like statues with their heads tilted to the side, one eye toward the sky, or take shelter under the rhododendrons.

When our friends started hearing that we could communicate on a basic level with our flock, they probably thought we were a little crazy. We decided we had to test our abilities with another flock. As a friend's flock roamed on her lawn, we started out with, "Hello (*buh-dup*)!" The chickens were bewildered at first and cocked their heads curiously. We could only think that for them it was like meeting an alien for the first time!

We spent about 20 minutes getting to know one another in this new way. Then the real test came. I sounded the alarm. Immediately, the head hen acknowledged my warning and, amazingly, repeated the alarm. The whole flock froze with their heads tilted up and one eye on the sky. That day we discovered that chicken chat is universal!

What Is That Chicken Doing?

Chickens have natural behaviors that may seem strange to you at first. Almost from the very beginning, your flock will develop a social structure called the pecking order. Interestingly, the pecking order exists only within a group of hens. The rooster is usually exempt and is considered the ultimate boss. He protects his flock from predators, breaks up arguments among the hens, and constantly tries to impress his ladies. He will also fight with other roosters to maintain his status among them.

At the top of the pecking order is the head hen. Below her rank all the other hens, each in her own place. The head hen is often the first to eat or enjoy treats. She determines where the flock travels when free-ranging. Watch carefully and you will soon be able to establish who fits in where. When a hen who is below another hen in the flock tries to assert herself, the higher-up hen will usually give her a warning peck on the back of the neck.

When a hen dies or you add more chickens to the flock, you might see some fighting among the hens as they reestablish the pecking order. This is all normal behavior and it can last for a few weeks until a new order is established.

One chicken serves as the lookout. This is her main job and she does it every day. This chicken scans the skies and space surrounding them for signs of danger and issues a warning when necessary. This job is usually reserved for the roosters, but if no rooster is present, a hen will take on the role. In our flock, Sunshine fills this role.

Sunshine has hopped up on this stump and is alert to some strange noise. See her open beak? She's telling the others to watch out for possible danger.

Watch This!

Here are some other chicken behaviors that you will observe over time:

Exploring. Chickens are naturally curious. They love to wander around and explore their surroundings, even off-limit places!

Laying eggs. A laying hen sits in a nesting box to lay her eggs. The process can take an hour or so.

Scratching. Chickens spend a great deal of time scratching their feet in the earth to find food and explore new spots. This behavior is great exercise that also keeps their toenails trim.

Beak rubbing. Chickens often rub their beaks back and forth on a variety of surfaces including rocks, branches, logs, and the ground. This is to maintain the shape and length of their beaks as well as to clean them.

Pecking. Their beaks are a tool for eating and drinking, but chickens also use their beaks to explore their world. They are very curious and will peck at almost anything.

Roosting. Chickens feel safest when roosting up off the ground. It's a natural instinct to roost up away from predators. Free-ranging chickens without a coop will roost in trees at night.

Preening. After taking a dust bath, chickens restore the natural waterproofing oil in their feathers. They take oil from the uropygial gland located at the base of their tails and smooth it along each individual feather with their beaks.

Crowing. Roosters crow at any hour, not just dawn. They are warning the flock of predators, scaring off potential threats, and announcing their presence.

Alarm response. When the chicken on guard sounds the alarm, a low rolling growl, the entire flock will put one eye to the sky and freeze in place until the threat of danger is over.

Exploring Nature with Chickens

It's fun to just sit and watch your chickens interact with one another and the environment. Something is always going on. We call this "Chicken TV." We started tuning into Chicken TV when our first chicks were in the brooder. We would sit for a long time, watching the chicks with our legs folded, our elbows resting on our knees, and our chins perched in the palms of our hands.

Following your chickens around the yard can be just as entertaining! Without spooking her and without making her think that you are chasing her, follow a particular hen around and investigate what she is doing. Is she scratching in the dirt? What is she finding? How many worms does she pull? Does she find any grubs? How long before she moves on to another spot? Did another chicken call to her? Is she with a group or exploring on her own? Use the checklist on pages 96 and 97 to record the activities of your flock.

PLAYING IN THE GRASS

Chickens love eating grass. It is one of their favorite things, although long blades of grass aren't good for them, so ask your parents to keep the yard mowed fairly short if you allow your hens to explore outside their run. They especially enjoy the patches of delicious clover and other leaves laced among the blades. Why not spend some time searching with the chickens for four-leaf clovers? As you hunt, pick three-leaf clovers and feed them to the hens. It is great bonding time.

Hens also love dandelions. Do you also find it hard to resist blowing the seeds from the dried stems? I used to cringe when the kids would blow the poufy tops, imagining my pristine lawn becoming full of dandelions. Now I welcome them spreading the seeds. It only means more dandelions for the chickens to enjoy come spring. We are sowing dandelion crops for the chickens, not to mention that our honeybees also appreciate the early blossoms.

BUG HUNTING EXPEDITION

Our chickens are always curious when we dig in the garden. They love it when we turn up earthworms and will often begin to dig in the same spots as we are. We enjoy moving bits of earth slowly and deliberately with our shovels to see what we can uncover and share with the flock.

Turn over rocks, peek under leaves, and roll aside rotting logs to reveal lots of bugs. Worms, roly-poly bugs, beetles, and earthworms are all fair game in the world of chickens. If you like, use a magnifying glass to take a closer look at these delicious treats.

EGG HUNT

Chickens who spend most of their days free-ranging are notorious for laying clutches of eggs in inconspicuous spots. Sometimes, a hen may even go missing for weeks on end, only to emerge and return to the coop followed by a handful of baby chicks.

Hiding nests in secretive places is most likely a trait that has been born into the chickens; hunting for them seems like a trait that is born into most kids!

Sometimes a broody hen will hide her eggs in a secret spot, hoping to hatch them.

Egg hunts can stem from your own observations. In the warm weather of spring, chickens should return to hearty egg laying. Sometimes, it seems that you should have more eggs than you are harvesting. You may grow suspicious as you realize there must be a hidden nest somewhere.

You will need to launch an investigation. In the morning, let the chickens out to roam about the garden as usual, but watch them closely. Where do they like to go? Are there any bushes or shrubbery that they like to frequent?

You might find yourself crawling on all fours, searching under bushes and squeezing into tight spots that a grown-up can't reach. It is great fun when you discover a hen's hidden treasure. Unfortunately, you can't keep these treasures. They could have been hidden for weeks and it might be unsafe to eat them. It's always best to toss them.

BEHAVIOR CHECKLIST

Watch one hen to see if you can spot the following behaviors:

→ *Make copies of this page and fill one out for each member of your flock.*

NAME OF CHICKEN:

_____

EATING

What are her favorite treats?

_____

[ ] Scratching in the dirt

What type of bugs does she find?

_____

Worm count: _____ Bug count: _____

What else does she eat in the garden?

_____

LAYING AN EGG

[ ] Sitting in the nesting box

[ ] Announcing the arrival of an egg

GROOMING

[ ] Preening her feathers

[ ] Taking a dust bath

QUIET TIME

[ ] Taking a nap

Does she have a favorite hiding spot?

_____

DRINKING

How often does she take a drink? _____

SOCIALIZING

[ ] Chatting with another flock member

Who is her favorite chicken friend?

_____

Whom does she avoid? _____

Does she pick on any other hens? _____

What sounds does she make? _____

[ ] Interacting with people

Will she come for treats? _____

Does she let you pick her up? _____

Watch your flock as the seasons change. What changes do you notice in their behavior?

WINTER

How do they react to snow?

_____

→ Will they step on it? → Do they need you to
   YES   NO   shovel out a path?
                            YES   NO

How do they keep warm?

_____

Do they spend more time in the coop?

_____

Are they still laying eggs?   YES   NO
How many? _____

Did the number decrease?   YES   NO

What time do they put themselves to
bed, now that the days are shorter? _____

SUMMER

Do you notice signs of overheating?

→ Breathing through   → Holding wings away
   their mouths   from their bodies
   YES   NO   YES   NO

Do they chase after grasshoppers and
other insects?   YES   NO

Have they caught any salamanders
or frogs?   YES   NO

Who enjoys taking a nap in the sun?

_____

Do they have a favorite spot for a dust bath?

_____

SPRING

Are your older hens laying eggs again?
NO   YES   Date: _____

Is anyone broody? Who?

_____

As the days get longer, when do
they put themselves to bed? _____

How do they act when they see new
green leaves and shoots of grass?

_____

_____

What do they do when they
see a mud puddle?

_____

_____

FALL

When did they start molting? _____

→   Who is having the worst molt?

    _____

→   Who is molting the least?

    _____

Do they like scratching through piles
of leaves?   YES   NO

Put a small pumpkin in the run and
see who gives it the first peck. How
long does it take them to devour it?

_____

_____

97

Go to a Poultry Show!

Poultry shows are held across the country, often as part of county or state fairs. Attending them is a great family activity. They are good places to meet other kids who love chickens, to learn about breeds, and to see some really spectacular birds. You won't see only chickens, either — there will be competitions for ducks, turkeys, pigeons, and geese, too.

Visiting a show can be a good way to find new members for your flock. Look for an area where breeders sell all kinds of birds (and you can usually find bunnies, too!).

Attending your first poultry show can be a bit overwhelming, as you soon realize how many wonderful chicken breeds exist in the world. But though they might seem confusing at first, the shows are well organized.

WHAT TO EXPECT

Chickens are judged on a point system determined for each breed by the American Poultry Association (APA). The closer the chicken comes to the APA standard of perfection, the higher it will rank. A chicken may be disqualified from competition if it doesn't meet the standards.

Show chickens are separated into categories — first by size, either Large Fowl or Bantam. Next is by class. For Large Fowl, this is based on each breed's place of origin, such as the American Class. For Bantams, it is based on characteristics such as Feathered Legs. Every breed is listed in only one class.

Within each class, the chickens are separated by breed, such as Silkie Bantam or Rhode Island Red. The next division is the variety or color as defined in the standards of perfection. Some breeds come in colors that are not recognized by the APA.

At a poultry show, you can see many different breeds of chickens together in one place.

Showing chickens is a great way to learn a lot about them while having a good time.

Finally, the birds are separated by gender and age. Chickens can begin to be shown as early as about three months of age, or when their feathers are completely filled out.

In each class, the judges meticulously inspect each bird. Every chicken has to meet the requirements for conformation (body type) and feathering for its breed. An example of the standard for Silkie Bantams is that they must have dark eyes and five toes. Silkies born with only four toes, as sometimes happens, do not meet the showing standards, but they can be entered in showmanship.

WHAT IS SHOWMANSHIP?

A really good way to learn about chickens is to watch kids participating in the showmanship portion of a poultry show. Rather than judging the bird, the judge is interested in seeing how much you know about poultry and how well you handle your bird. The judges take their time to really work with kids during their first few times participating. Kids as young as age six can participate.

Typically the judge has all the kids line up with their birds at the showmanship table. One by one, the judge chats with each kid about chickens. The judge asks questions about care and handling, as well as general poultry facts.

After the individual questioning, the judge asks the group to show various parts of their birds. At the end, the judge awards ribbons for first through fifth place.

SHOWING YOUR OWN CHICKENS

A great way to start showing chickens is to get involved in your local 4-H club. Often you can find a mentor to help you select your birds, practice handling your chickens with you, and teach you about participating in shows.

If you are younger than 18, you will most likely be in the junior division rather than the open division, which is for all ages. As a junior you can enter a showmanship class or show your birds on their merits, or both.

To participate in showmanship, you don't need a show-quality chicken, only a chicken who is tame and cooperative. If you choose to show your chicken in other classes, you will need a bird whose breed is recognized by the APA.

Kids participating in showmanship are required to dress neatly, usually in a white shirt with khaki, white, or black pants.

WHY I LOVE CHICKENS!

ALEXIS, Age 13, Killingly, Connecticut

Alexis and her mother, Pam, show their "Sensational Silkies by Blake" across New England.

How old were you when you got chickens?
When I was 11, my parents picked me up at summer camp and surprised me by driving in the opposite direction of home to pick up 12 pet-quality chicks. After we brought them home, they grew up to be something we never thought possible: actual pets!

When you sat in the run, five would jump onto your lap all at once. Cuddles, our favorite, had to be on your shoulder at all times, whether you wanted her there or not. What we once saw as a strange, smelly creature, commonly consumed for dinner, was now part of the family.

How did you learn about showing chickens?
My mother saw an ad for chicken diapers. When she looked it up, thinking it was hysterical (which it was), she found something else: chicken shows. We just couldn't resist exploring something that sounded so insane. What we didn't know was we were soon to be a proud part of that insanity.

I guess our interactions with them made us want to find a way to have even more fun — I mean, somebody had to show off these beauties!

Why did you choose Silkies to raise and show?
Who wouldn't want those colorful balls of fluff waddling around their yard all day? They are really adorable and have absolutely great personalities. It

was a perfect fit for a first-time chicken-owning family who didn't have a clue.

We bought our first birds, but now we breed our own. Once every few generations, we may purchase a few really nice hens or a handsome rooster to add new bloodlines. We have a flock of 70 beautiful birds who hold a very special place in our hearts. We also have four Seramas, another small breed that is ideal for showmanship.

What's the best way for kids to start?
At first, I enjoyed just looking at the other breeds. Some are very strange! Kids usually start in the juniors division where they don't have to worry that they won't do well, because the classes are more for fun. Who cares if you win or not? You just keep getting better each time.

Beginners shouldn't show in the adult division because the judges are much more strict and the exhibitors are extremely competitive. Judges aren't very hard on the juniors. Showing in juniors also gains you more ribbons, which is always a plus.

Do you have to have show-quality birds?
You do if you're looking to take home ribbons in the show category. If you're in it for fun and to gain experience, bring in the cutest runt you have! Just don't feel defeated if the judge disqualifies your bird.

Now, the showmanship class is completely different. Your bird can have a crossed beak or no feathers, or be small, skinny, tall, or chubby — nobody cares in showmanship. You just need to be able to handle the bird properly.

But if you have a beautiful bird, you can enter it in a breed class and compete in showmanship at the same show.

What might a judge ask?
The instructor will ask the kids to do certain things like show their birds' wings, vent, uropygial gland (or preening gland), and other parts. One of my personal favorites is the "popsicle," where the handler is asked to hold the bird's legs firmly together so that the bird calmly stays upright.

What is the highest level of award one of your chickens has received?
One of my chickens won the reserve grand champion in juniors, meaning second best bird at the junior show. It was a proud moment for me, and also for the bird, who went through an unwanted spa treatment and was put into a foreign setting, but still pulled through.

What lessons have you learned?
Don't bring a broody hen or one that will try to bite the judge's hand off. Always bring more food than you need and bring a bottle of aspirin if you get headaches easily. It's always better to be over-prepared than under. That's the best advice I can give.

HOW TO BATHE A CHICKEN

Certain members of your flock may have a difficult time keeping their fluffy bottoms clean despite their daily dust baths. Soiled bottoms can result from an infection or just loose stools from something in the diet.

Most chickens can benefit from a bath once in a while, but chickens who attend poultry shows are always bathed before the show. An egg-bound hen can also benefit from a soak in warm water and Epsom salts. Whether you show your birds or not, you may want to learn how to bathe a chicken.

SUPPLIES

- Three old bath towels
- Two bins or bowls large enough to hold a chicken
- Warm water
- Dawn dish detergent or other gentle brand. Pet shampoo works also.
- A plastic cup
- Hair dryer

SETUP

Before collecting your chicken, prepare your bathing area.

→ Spread out a couple of towels for the containers.

→ Fill both containers halfway with warm water and add a few drops of detergent to one of them. Mix the soap to create some bubbles.

→ Make a drying station on a table away from the water. Lay out a towel and plug in the hair dryer.

DIRECTIONS

1. If you think that a chicken will be nervous during her first bath, you can cover her entire head with a small towel to help keep her calm. Place the chicken in the bin with the soapy water. Use the cup and your hands to wet the soiled area.

   Once the feathers are wet, gently rub the dirty feathers with your fingers. Make sure any hardened-on poop is soft before you try to pick it off. Do not be afraid to clean right around the vent.

2. When the chicken is clean, transfer her to the second basin and rinse the soap off completely. Slide your hands down her body to remove the excess water.

Remember to keep talking to your chicken during the entire process. The sound of your voice will reassure her.

3. Wrap her in a towel to absorb more water. She'll probably be happy to have her head uncovered by now!

4. With the dryer set on warm (not hot!) and low, dry the wet feathers. You may need to keep her wings wrapped in a towel to keep her from flapping. Keep the dryer moving continuously until the chicken is completely dry, which should take about 5 minutes.

5. When you're done, you'll be amazed at how fluffy a clean chicken can be!

10 CHICKENS IN THE GARDEN

Many people who keep chickens also have flower or vegetable gardens, and they soon discover that their chickens adore exploring the yard and investigating the garden beds.

We love to see those fluffy butts scratching in the compost pile, digging through fallen leaves, and resting under shady hosta leaves. Our chickens make our gardens come alive with energy, happiness, and color!

Gardening with chickens is great fun. One thing to realize, however, is that chickens in the garden often lack manners and have little impulse control. They can't tell the difference between your vegetable seedlings and the garden you planted just for them. They devour fresh baby plants and nibble on lush leaves. They scatter mulch and tear up the lawn. They take dust baths in your flower beds, and they poop everywhere! You will need to teach them how to behave.

As chickens scratch to their heart's content, mulch and dirt fly everywhere! It's easy to rake up after they move on to a new area.

Sprouts

Chickens love greens, but they are not always available year-round from the garden. Growing sprouts is a fun, easy way to provide your flock with greens. Sprouts are a great source of vitamins, minerals, omega-3 fatty acids, and fiber. You can find them at a health food store, but it's much less expensive to sprout your own seeds and grains.

Here are some seeds and grains to try:

- Alfalfa
- Beet
- Broccoli
- Fenugreek
- Microgreens
- Pea
- Radish
- Sunflower
- Wheat berry

SUPPLIES

Wide-mouth 1-quart canning jar
Sprouting lid or cheesecloth
Large rubber band
Seeds
Water

1. Put 1 or 2 tablespoons of seeds in the canning jar. Cover the mouth of the jar with the sprouting cover or cheesecloth. Rinse the seeds with water and drain them, then add enough water to cover the seeds and let them sit overnight.

2. Drain the seeds in the morning, then rinse and drain them again. Tilt or lay the jar full of seeds on its side in a warm spot with indirect sunlight, such as a windowsill. For the next few days, rinse the seeds and drain them completely two or three times per day. They need to be kept moist but not wet.

3. Seeds should begin to sprout in a few days. Continue to rinse and drain them a couple of times per day. Your sprouts are ready when their leaves turn green.

Chickens also love microgreens. You can grow some microgreens using the sprout jar technique or in seedling trays with soil. If you grow them in soil, simply snip the seedlings off with scissors as they get their first two sets of leaves. The seed package should have detailed growing directions.

CHUNNEL
(A Chicken Tunnel)

When I first heard the idea of making tunnels for chickens, I was smitten! These movable wire tubes, often called *chunnels*, allow chickens to safely enjoy a little extra freedom. Chunnels are very practical if you want to restrict access to flower beds or a vegetable garden. They offer some protection from predators and allow your chickens controlled access to grassy and wooded areas. They provide an easy way to move chickens from one location to another such as between two coop setups. The best part is that they come together easily and can be taken apart in little time.

WHAT YOU NEED

- ½-inch hardware cloth, 3 to 4 feet wide and in your desired lengths
- Ground staples used with pet fence installation
- Rubber mallet
- Wire cutters
- Cable ties

What You Do

1. Determine the path you want to create with the chunnels.

2. Bend the hardware cloth into a half circle and secure it to the ground with ground staples using the mallet. Repeat on the other side.

3. Build the tunnels as long as you want, overlapping the sections of wire slightly and connecting them with the cable ties.

4. Train your chickens to use the chunnels by enticing them inside with a few mealworms.

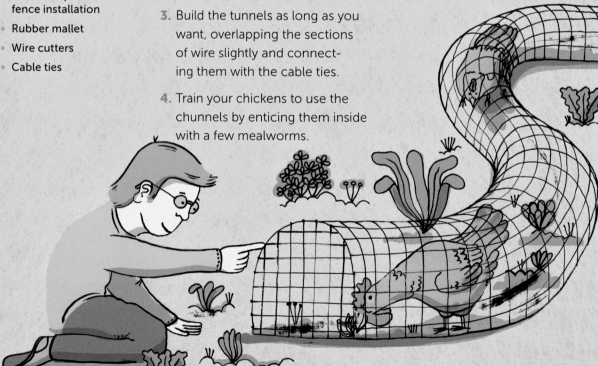

Establish the Rules

When your chickens are free in the garden, they will need to be supervised. Chickens will follow you around the garden, especially when you dig. They are curious and eager to see what your shovel or pitchfork might turn up for them to eat. But they will also wander all over the place to see what sort of trouble they can find!

You can teach them to forage in areas that are acceptable. Coax them away from off-limit areas by gently shooing them to a new area. Toss down some chicken scratch, a mix of cracked corn and barley or wheat, in the chicken-friendly zones.

You can also plant the area right around the coop just for the chickens. Provide chicken-safe plants in an area where they can scratch, eat, and explore to their hearts' content. This might encourage them to stay where you want them to.

Consider corralling the flock with small fenced-off areas accessible via chunnels.

If you have garden beds or other areas where you do not want the chickens to go, you might need to put fences around them or make chicken-wire cages to surround off-limit plants, seedlings, and new plantings.

Digging up worms and bugs is a cool way to interact with your flock.

When the chickens are in the garden, leave the coop door open. They will return to lay eggs, have a snack, take a drink, and check in once in a while. You don't need to watch them every minute, but do keep an eye on them, especially when they are just starting out exploring. As the sun sets, instinct tells them to head home to roost, and they naturally "tuck themselves into bed."

Chunnels are not 100 percent predator-proof, especially to digging animals. Take time to peek at your flock now and then when the chunnels are in use.

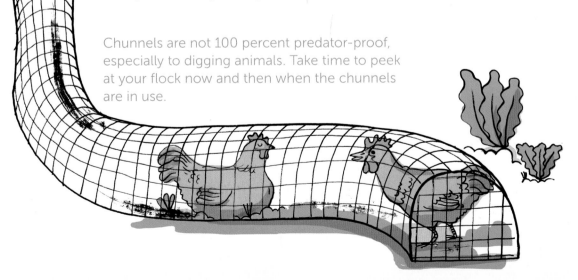

A CHICKEN-FRIENDLY GARDEN

Left to their own devices, chickens can make a mess when they are free-ranging. Along with weeds, they will eat your prized vegetables and perennials. A few rogue chickens can destroy a vegetable garden in the blink of an eye. So why not plant some tempting treats near the chicken coop, just for the flock?

You don't even have to create a whole garden — you can start with a few herbs in containers. The chickens love it when you rotate these containers into the run. When one container starts to look too raggedy, swap in the other one.

As long as the chickens do not eat all the leaves from the plant, your herbs will continue to grow back throughout the season. Some herbs can live for years in a container, if they are properly cared for.

BEE BALM

CATMINT

CATNIP

CHAMOMILE

CHIVE

CILANTRO

DILL

LAVENDER

LEMON VERBENA

MINT

OREGANO

THYME

EDIBLE HERB WREATH

Chickens love herbs, and we love creating entirely edible wreaths for our flock. They are decorative and fragrant, at least before the hens gobble them all up!

You can use any combination of herbs or flowers; this one is made with lavender, one of our flock's favorites. Each wreath is unique and beautiful, and you can easily make another one. It's a wonderful present to give your flock.

WHAT YOU NEED

- **Large bunch of fresh or dried herb sprigs or cut flowers**
- Scissors
- Garden twine
- One 8-inch box-wired wreath form

TIP: Try using some of the herbs found on page 109. Our girls especially love lavender, oregano, bee balm, sunflowers, chamomile, and mint.

What You Do

1. Cut a number of 6-inch lengths of twine.

2. Lay stems together, lining up the blossoms or tops of the sprigs, to make a bundle about 4 inches wide.

3. Tie the bundle together approximately 5 inches below the top. Cut off the excess stems about 1 inch below the twine.

4. Tie the bundle to the wreath form.

5. Continue making bundles and tying them to the wreath form in a counterclockwise direction. Add extra lengths of twine to secure the bundles as necessary.

6. Once the wreath is completely filled, flip it over and tuck in any loose pieces of twine.

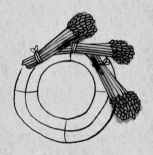

Top Garden Plants for Chickens

In addition to herbs, chickens love lots of other plants. The plants discussed here are easy to grow and provide good food for you as well as for your chickens.

→ Beet greens are full of vitamins and minerals such as vitamin C, manganese, folate, magnesium, potassium, and iron. Beets are a fabulous cold-weather crop, growing nicely in the spring and fall. They come in many different varieties ranging from the traditional dark fuchsia color to yellow to pink with white stripes. When you are ready to harvest the beets, the chickens will gladly eat the stems and leaves that you toss aside.

→ Broccoli flowers, stems, and leaves are another welcome treat for the flock. Did you know that the broccoli we eat is actually the flower before it blooms? Your flock enjoys the entire plant, and they do not mind if the broccoli has begun to "bolt," or to make yellow flowers. Eating the leaves and tougher stems keeps them busy for a while and helps to bust boredom.

→ Carrots are another easy-to-grow chicken favorite. Every year, my kids are amazed at how tiny these seeds are! Carrots grow best when the seeds are planted directly into the ground. As you thin them out, share the discards with the chickens, no matter how tiny.

The carrots will grow the entire summer and be ready for an early fall harvest. During the harvest, we share the carrot tops and any carrots that were nibbled on by pests. You can toss the entire carrot into the run, greens and all!

CHICKEN SCHOOL

Cherish Your Friends

One thing we've learned about chickens that has surprised us is that they seem capable of caring for one another. Having friends is important to people, and chickens seem to have friends, too.

At first, we thought that it wouldn't matter if a chicken was missing from the flock, but it sure does! One flock member keeps tabs on the others. As soon as the scout chicken realizes someone is missing, she'll call out as if to say, "Here we are, over here." Almost immediately, the missing chicken comes running to reunite with the flock.

Some chickens seem to have a definite preference for who they hang out with, and they may form particularly close relationships. Our Buff Orpingtons, Oyster Cracker and Sunshine, spend most of their time within a wingspan of each other.

When one is laying an egg, the other paces outside the nesting box. They cackle back and forth, as though checking on the progress. After the egg song rings out, they go back to hanging out together, looking for tasty treats or having a dust bath.

→ Greens, such as mustard greens, kale, cabbage, chard, and lettuce, are crops that chickens love. They grow very fast and are hardy. Like the herbs, you can also plant these greens in containers. This is a great way to make the garden portable!

→ Berries. Chickens love all berries, and we share our blueberries, strawberries, blackberries, and raspberries with them. Many varieties of berries can be planted in the ground or in containers. Chickens also happily snack on apples, pears, plums (pits removed), and peaches (pits removed).

→ Nasturtiums are a wonderful, easy-to-grow annual. The entire plant is edible, from its stems to its yellow, orange, and red blossoms. It has a peppery taste. Nasturtiums come in many different varieties. Some climb, while others are bush-like.

They attract beneficial bugs to your gardens and keep unwanted pests like squash bugs, cucumber beetles, and caterpillars away. Nasturtiums are a great source of vitamin C and are also possibly helpful in preventing worms in your flock. This is our flock's favorite! It never takes long for the girls to notice once we plant a few seedlings around the chicken run.

→ Sunflower seeds are divine! Did you know that as the sun moves across the sky in the day, the blooms follow along? As the stems grow taller they may require some support from staking. In the late summer, cut the blooms from the plant and set them aside to dry the delicious seeds. Sunflower seeds are rich in protein, and their harvest time perfectly coincides with the flock's annual molt.

WEEDS ARE WONDERFUL!

Whether you welcome weeds to your yard or you despise them, one thing is for sure: chickens love them. They are sought-after treats that also attract bees and other pollinators, so we have come to embrace plants such as clover, plantain, lamb's-quarter, dandelion, chickweed, and purslane as part of our lawn.

If your folks just can't stand them, offer to dig them out of the lawn and toss them into the chicken run for the chickens, roots and all.

Composting with Chickens

Composting is a simple and earth-friendly way to turn waste from your chickens and kitchen into black gold for your garden. The process starts with combining "green material" and "brown material" (see below) with some water and heat. Soon, beneficial bugs, worms, and microbes find your compost pile a desirable place to live. They help break down the green and brown material into smaller and smaller pieces, producing beautiful compost to enrich your garden soil.

You can start a compost pile on the ground or in a bin. Locate it where it will receive a good deal of sun during the day and is easy to reach so that you can toss material in it frequently. As you add to the compost pile, strive for six inches of brown to three inches of green. A great way to add brown to your green is by cleaning out the chicken coop. Pine shavings easily add to the amount of brown! Note that chicken manure is high in ammonia, so never use it directly in the garden as it can kill your plants.

It is important for your compost pile to stay moist but not soggy. Add water as necessary to create a moist environment for those beneficial microbes. Turning your compost pile with a pitchfork now and then will help to speed up the process.

Compost piles should not smell bad. If yours begins to smell, it could be from being too wet or having too much "green." Try adding more "brown" to obtain a better balance of ingredients.

Green Material (protein for microbes)

- → Chicken manure
- → Coffee grounds with filter and tea bags
- → Fresh green grass clippings
- → Fresh green leaves and yard waste
- → Kitchen scraps such as fruit and vegetable trimmings, eggshells, bread

Brown Material (carbon for energy)

- → Cardboard
- → Dry yellow and brown leaves
- → Dryer lint
- → Pine shavings
- → Egg cartons
- → Shredded newspaper
- → Small amounts of wood ash
- → Straw
- → Woody plant stalks

11 CHICKEN CRAFTS

My kids love to craft — it's a great way to unplug from electronics, television, and the phone and to be creative, especially on rainy or cold days. Let your imagination come alive as you share ideas and invent new creations.

We do all our crafting at the kitchen table. We spread out newspaper or craft paper and bring out a variety of materials, along with scissors, glue, and tape. We always have a few extra egg cartons on hand, too. Here is a basic list that you can add to:

→ Acrylic paints

→ Paintbrushes in different sizes

→ Markers and crayons

→ Felt squares and fabric remnants

→ Feathers

→ Googly eyes

→ Pipe cleaners

→ Scissors

→ Craft glue

HOW TO BLOW OUT AND DECORATE EGGS

We love to decorate eggs for Easter. Most folks hard-boil the eggs before they dye them and then store them in the refrigerator so they don't spoil. Others leave the hard-boiled eggs out for display, but then they are not safe to eat.

By blowing the raw egg out of the shells, you can decorate your eggs without wasting the insides. But if you want to use traditional dye for your eggs, do so prior to blowing them out. Otherwise, your eggs will float on top of the dye.

If your flock lays colored eggs, you may want to keep them natural rather than dyeing them. For decorating, you can use traditional dyes or mix it up by drawing on the shells with waterproof markers or decoupaging them with paper or fabric cutouts or shreds of colored tissue paper. When not displayed, store your eggs in egg cartons to enjoy them year after year.

Here's an easy way to blow out eggs (they should be at room temperature before you start).

You'll need a small nail (like a picture-hanging brad), a spoon, a nasal syringe, some distilled white vinegar, a bowl, and a large pot.

1. Starting at the skinnier end of the egg, gently tap the nail into the eggshell with the back of the spoon. Be sure to puncture the membrane just under the shell. Repeat on the wider end. Use the nail to widen each hole to approximately the size of a dulled pencil tip.

2. Holding the egg over a bowl, place the nasal syringe over one of the holes and gently blow air through the egg to force out the contents. Keep blowing air through until the egg is empty. Repeat this process until you have blown out as many eggs as you need.

3. Fill a pot with 10 parts water and 1 part distilled white vinegar. Pressing the blown-out eggs into the liquid, allow them to fill up with the water and vinegar solution to clean them. Blow the water out of the eggs with the syringe and set them aside to dry.

Decorating with felt-tip markers is quick and easy, but don't stop there. Try dyeing, painting, and decoupage, or come up with your own creative scheme.

115

EGG CARTON TREASURE BOXES

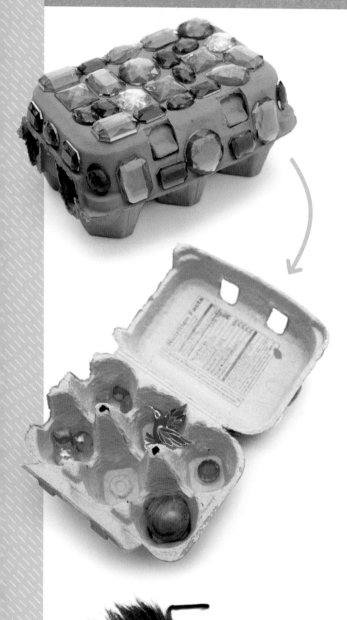

Like most kids, you probably love collecting miniature things such as figurines, coins, pressed pennies, erasers, and shells. These boxes are perfect for keeping tiny treasures safe in one spot. You can make several and decorate them lots of different ways. How about a pirate or fairy theme?

WHAT YOU NEED

- Newspaper/craft paper
- Cardboard egg cartons, 6- or 12-egg size
- Acrylic craft paint
- Paintbrushes
- Crafting glue or hot glue gun
- Decorating supplies (gems, pompoms, pipe cleaners, feathers, whatever you like)

What You Do

1. Spread the paper across your crafting space.

2. Paint your egg cartons and allow them to dry completely.

3. Glue on your decorations.

4. Fill your box up with treasures!

A hairy spider makes a good disguise for a treasure box!

EGG CARTON WIND CHIME

Here's an unusual way to use a couple of egg cartons. This craft is especially wonderful when you hang it in front of a window. The bells that are tucked inside the egg cups make a lovely sound as the mobile moves in the breeze. These mobiles are also a lovely gift idea for the holidays.

WHAT YOU NEED

- Newspaper/craft paper
- Cardboard egg carton
- Acrylic paint, assorted colors
- Paintbrushes
- Scissors or small hole punch
- 12 small metal bells (½-inch diameter)
- Brown garden twine
- Slender branch approximately 16 inches long

Hang your chimes in front of an open window to bring them to life.

What You Do

1. Spread the newspaper out on your work space. Cut the egg carton into 12 separate cups.

2. Paint the cups — it's fun to use different colors for the outside and the inside. Set them aside to dry.

3. Make a small slit or X on the top of each cup with scissors, or use the hole punch. Cut three pieces of string at least 3 feet long.

4. Tie a bell onto the end of a piece of string. Thread the other end of the string through the bottom of an egg cup, so that it slides down over the bell.

5. Tie a second bell onto the string 6 to 8 inches above the first one, and thread another egg cup over it. Repeat until the string is full, then make two more strings in the same way.

6. Hang the strings from the branch. Tie a string handle onto the branch to hang your creation in a window or by your chicken coop!

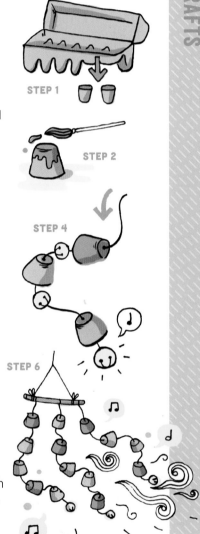

STEP 1

STEP 2

STEP 4

STEP 6

NOTE: Use more egg cartons and bells to make your wind chime as full of sound as you want. You can also cut shapes, such as triangles or rounded flower petals, onto the edges of your egg cups or punch holes in the sides to make a pattern.

117

BLOOMING LOLLIPOPS

These are great fun to bring to school to celebrate the holidays or the first day of spring, or just as a different way to treat your friends. You can even make an edible bouquet!

WHAT YOU NEED

- Cardboard egg cartons
- Scissors
- Newspaper/craft paper
- Acrylic craft paint
- Paintbrushes
- Colored tissue paper
- Toothpick
- Hot glue gun and glue sticks
- Lollipops

What You Do

1. Cut the egg carton into 12 separate cups.

2. Cut petal shapes into the top edges of each cup. You can round them or keep them straight, or try to make them pointy.

3. Spread paper on your work surface, then paint the cups inside and out. Set them aside to dry.

4. Cut several dozen circles from the tissue paper, approximately 4 inches in diameter.

5. Carefully poke a hole with the toothpick through the center of a few tissue paper circles and through the center of the bottom of an egg cup.

6. Slide several paper circles onto a lollipop stick, then push the stick through the bottom of an egg cup, as shown. The fit should be snug. If it's too loose, use a dab of hot glue to secure it.

STEP 1

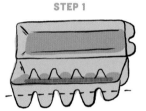

STEP 2

STEP 3

STEP 6

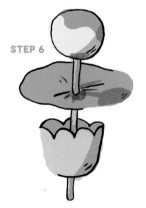

118

DECORATED EGG HOLDERS

Use these cute egg holders to show off fancy decorated eggs or to display a variety of fresh eggs from your flock. You can even paint them to look like your favorite hen.

What You Do

1. Cut an egg carton on the diagonal so that you wind up with a center divider and two cups that are across from each other, not side by side (see diagram). You can cut 5 egg holders out of one carton. Spread out your newspaper, and paint the egg cups. Set them aside to dry.

2. To decorate your chicken, glue on some feathers for the tail and wings. Cut pieces of felt for the comb and wattles and glue them on. Cut a diamond shape from the felt, fold it in half to make a beak, and glue it into place. Last, add some eyes with markers or glue on a pair of googly eyes.

3. Once the glue is dry, load your chicken up with a couple of eggs.

WHAT YOU NEED

- Cardboard egg cartons
- Acrylic paints
- Paintbrushes
- Newspaper/craft paper
- Felt
- Craft glue
- Markers
- Googly eyes
- Scissors
- Feathers
- Pipe cleaners
- Hole punch

FOR A FUN TWIST, add some pipe cleaner legs to your flock of chickens. Make a set of legs and feet with yellow or orange pipe cleaners. With a small hole punch, make two holes on the base of the chicken's body, insert the pipe cleaners, and twist them into place.

Collect feathers from your own flock to use on your creations.

119

HOW TO DRAW A CHICKEN

Drawing chickens is fun and easy. Here's a simple, step-by-step method to practice with. Sketch in pencil so you can make changes easily.

1. Draw two ovals, one for the body and one for the head.

2. Add the neck and tail.

3. Add the legs, feet, and wings.

4. Add the wattles, comb, beak, and eyes.

5. Fill in the feathering and final details.

6. Go over your sketch in ink, if you want, and color it in. Erase any extra pencil marks. Put your favorite drawing in a frame!

If you want to draw a detailed picture of a chicken, try this simple trick: Start with a photo. For one thing, a photo will stay still while you draw.

And here's another cool trick: Turn the photo upside down and draw your picture while looking at the photo that way. When the photo is upside down, your brain will interpret the photo not as a chicken, but as lines and shapes that are easier for you to follow. Pretty amazing, isn't it?

CHICKEN PHOTOGRAPHY

One thing that you will soon realize is that when it comes to taking their photos, chickens are incredibly fast! They do not sit still for anyone. Their heads seem to be constantly moving, and just when they pose and you grab the camera, they are off to the next best thing. Don't give up! It is possible to get some really stunning photos of your flock. Here are some things to know.

→ Start with a good digital camera that has zooming capabilities and various automatic photo-taking modes.

→ Learn to love the sports mode. It helps to catch things that are constantly moving.

→ Bribery will get you everywhere! Chickens love treats and they don't mind standing in one place while eating. Sprinkle some scratch on the ground and then snap away.

→ Always take more photos than you think you will need or want. Lots of them won't come out quite the way you hoped.

→ Take your photos outdoors in the daylight. Natural light is the best.

→ Focus on just one chicken, and watch her through your lens until you like the shot. Use the zoom and fill up most of the frame before you snap your photo.

→ Try to tell a story or convey what your chickens were doing when you took the photo. This makes the pictures much more interesting.

→ Don't forget to have someone take a few photos of you with your flock, too!

CHICKEN COIN PURSE

Everyone loves to have a little place to tuck their coins and secret treasures. These small, handheld felt chickens are the perfect guardians to keep your goodies safe!

WHAT YOU NEED

- Tracing paper
- Assorted felt squares, 9" × 12" (red, yellow, and brown or other color for body)
- Scissors
- Fabric glue
- Embroidery floss
- Needle, large eye
- Two small craft eyes, shank-back type (or use googly eyes for a silly chicken)
- Iron-on Velcro (narrow tape or small dots)

What You Do

1. Copy the pattern pieces on the facing page onto tracing paper and cut them out. Trace the pattern onto the felt and cut out the pieces.

2. Glue the wings to the body first, then fold the lower body part up to form a little pouch. Glue along the edges as shown. Set aside until the glue is dry.

3. Stitch around the edges of the pouch with the embroidery floss to reinforce the glue.

4. Cut two small pieces of Velcro or use two dots. Following the directions on the package, iron them into place as shown. This will keep your coin purse closed.

5. Glue the comb, beak, and tail feathers to the pouch. Let it dry thoroughly before the next step.

6. Attach the eyes according to the directions on the package, or glue on googly eyes.

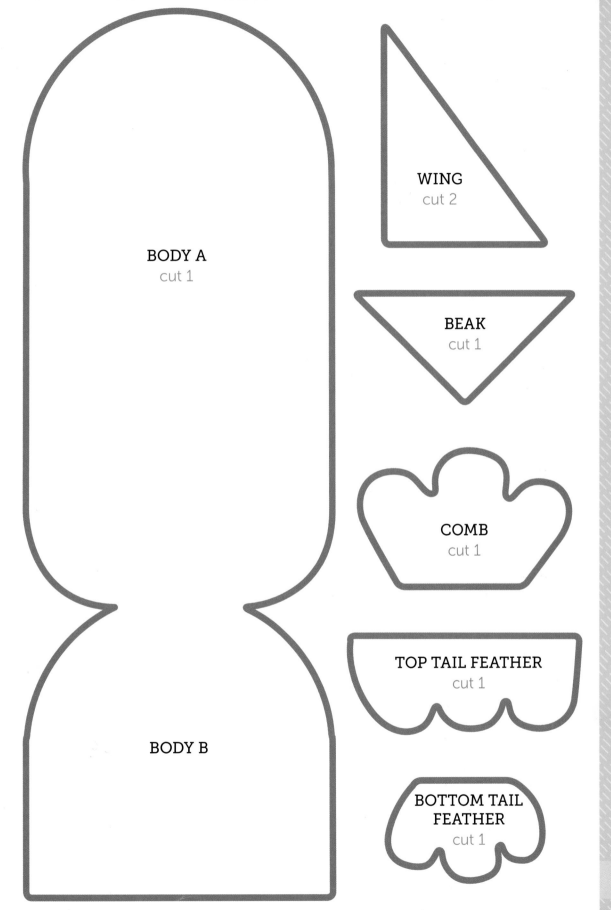

BODY A
cut 1

BODY B

WING
cut 2

BEAK
cut 1

COMB
cut 1

TOP TAIL FEATHER
cut 1

BOTTOM TAIL
FEATHER
cut 1

12 COOKING WITH EGGS

Cooking with eggs is easy, and the recipes presented here are geared for simplicity. You will not need many ingredients. They are easy for kids to make with supervision, and they are a great way to learn the art of cooking.

You can enjoy these dishes any time of the day. You can make quiches, frittatas, and soups to have eggs wind up on your dinner plate. And, of course, there's always dessert!

When you cook, remember to keep things tidy, wash your hands with soap and water before you start and after handling raw eggs, and always have an adult supervising your creations. Let's start cooking!

1, 2, 3 WAYS TO COOK AN EGG

The first thing to learn about cooking eggs is how to make these basic styles.

HARD-BOILED

Once you've made hard-boiled eggs, you can do all sorts of things with them. Older eggs are easier to peel because they have a larger air pocket.

1. Put the uncooked eggs in a large pot of cold water. Be sure they are not crowded. Cover the eggs entirely with water.

2. Slowly bring the eggs to a gentle simmer (not a full boil). Simmer the eggs for 8 minutes.

3. Take the pot off the heat, put on the lid, and let the eggs rest in the water for 15 minutes.

4. Remove the eggs from the water and run them under cold water.

5. Keep hard-boiled eggs in the fridge for up to 7 days. It's a good idea to mark them somehow so you don't mistake an uncooked egg for a cooked one!

SCRAMBLED

Scrambled eggs is one of the easiest dishes to learn to cook. Try adding shredded cheese, crumbled cooked bacon, and/or chopped sautéed veggies to them for a fancier version!

1. Break two or three eggs into a bowl and mix them well with a whisk or fork. You can add up to ¼ cup of milk.

2. Heat a small to medium pan (depending on the number of eggs) over medium heat. Put a small pat of butter in the pan to melt while it heats up.

3. Spread the butter around, and pour the eggs into the pan all at once. Let them sit for a minute before stirring them with a spoon or spatula.

4. Let the eggs cook, stirring occasionally, until they form fluffy lumps. They cook fast, so pay attention the whole time! Take them off the heat when they reach the desired consistency.

FRIED

Fried eggs are a little trickier than scrambled, especially if you want to flip them, but practice makes perfect!

1. Heat a small frying pan over medium heat. Put a small pat of butter in the pan to melt while it heats up.

2. Carefully break your egg into the middle of the pan.

3. Let it cook for a few minutes, until the clear part (the albumen) turns white and the edges begin to brown.

4. If you like a sunny-side-up egg, you're done! For over easy, slide a spatula under the egg and carefully flip it over. Let it cook for a minute or two longer, depending on how runny you want the yolk to be.

French Toast

We love French toast for breakfast! It is an easy dish to make and will help you learn basic cooking skills such as cracking eggs, whisking, and using a spatula. For a special treat, try topping the French toast with fresh berries and whipped cream.

SERVES 4

INGREDIENTS

- 3 eggs
- ½ cup milk
- 1 teaspoon vanilla extract
- 2 tablespoons butter, plus more as needed
- 8 thick slices bread, cut in half
  Cinnamon

Instructions

1. Whisk together the eggs, milk, and vanilla in a small bowl.

2. Melt 2 tablespoons of butter in a large skillet over medium heat. Spread the butter over the entire cooking surface.

3. Dip several slices of bread into the egg mixture, coating both sides, and put them in the pan without crowding them. Sprinkle with cinnamon.

4. Cook the slices on one side until golden brown, then flip them with a spatula and cook until golden brown, about 2 minutes per side.

5. Add more slices as space in the pan becomes available. Add more butter to the pan as needed to prevent sticking.

Fancy Egg-in-the-Hole

This simple dish can be fancied up if you use cookie cutters of various shapes to cut the holes in the bread. It's fun to use seasonal cookie cutters for the holidays. My kids love it when snowmen show up to breakfast!

SERVES 2

INGREDIENTS

- 2 slices bread
- 2 tablespoons butter
- 2 eggs
  Salt and pepper

Instructions

1. Place the bread on a cutting board. Press a cookie cutter into the center of each slice and remove the cut-out piece. (You can feed that part to the chickens. They love bread!)

2. Melt 2 tablespoons of butter in a skillet over medium heat.

3. Place the bread in the skillet; carefully crack an egg into the center of each cutout.

4. Sprinkle lightly with salt and pepper.

5. Cook the bread and egg until the bottom is golden brown. Flip it over with a spatula and repeat on the other side.

Sausage, Egg & Cheese Breakfast Casserole

Nothing in the world starts off the day like a breakfast casserole. The eggs are light and fluffy and so delicious. The kids and I created this casserole, which has all of our favorite breakfast foods rolled into one dish. Sometimes we even have this one for dinner. It's delicious with your favorite hot sauce!

SERVES 6

INGREDIENTS

    Cooking spray
 1 pound ground breakfast sausage
 1 small onion, diced
 ½ green pepper, diced
 ½ red pepper, diced
 1 pound frozen shredded hash browns
 6 eggs
 1 cup milk
    Salt and pepper
 1 cup shredded cheddar cheese

Instructions

1. Preheat the oven to 375°F/190°C. Spray a casserole dish with cooking spray.

2. Cook the sausage, onions, and peppers in a skillet over medium heat until the sausage is browned, the peppers are tender, and the onions are translucent. Drain off the fat. Spoon the cooked mixture into a medium bowl and set aside.

3. Brown the hash browns in the same skillet. Meanwhile, whisk together the eggs and milk in a large mixing bowl. Add salt and pepper to taste.

4. Spread the hash browns on the bottom of the dish. Layer the sausage, peppers, and onions on top and sprinkle with half the cheese. Pour the egg mixture on top of the casserole and sprinkle with the remaining cheese.

5. Bake for approximately 30 minutes, until the eggs are cooked through and the cheese is melted and turning brown.

Apple-Pecan Puffed Pancake

My sister introduced us to this yummy treat, often called a Dutch baby pancake, while I was visiting her in Seattle. I could not wait to get home and make one with my kids. They love the way it puffs up in the oven. This wonderful breakfast or dessert is perfect for impressing your friends' stomachs and their eyes!

SERVES 4 TO 6

INGREDIENTS

- ¾ cup whole milk
- 2 eggs
- 1 cup flour
- ½ tablespoon vanilla extract
- ½ teaspoon salt
- 2 tablespoons butter, plus more for pan
- 1 cup peeled and sliced apples
- ⅓ cup chopped pecans
- 2 tablespoons brown sugar
- 1 tablespoon white sugar
- 1 tablespoon lemon juice
- ½ teaspoon cinnamon
- ¼ teaspoon nutmeg
- Confectioners' sugar
- Maple syrup

Instructions

1. Preheat the oven to 400°F/205°C. Grease a pie plate with butter and set aside.

2. Whisk the milk, eggs, flour, vanilla, and salt in a medium bowl and set aside.

3. Melt the butter in a medium saucepan over medium heat. Add the apples and sauté until they begin to soften. Add the pecans, sugars, lemon juice, cinnamon, and nutmeg to the skillet and stir until melted and bubbly and the apples are tender.

4. Pour the apple mixture into the pie plate. Pour the batter on top of the apples and bake for approximately 25 minutes, until puffy and golden brown.

5. Dust with confectioners' sugar, cut into slices, and serve warm with maple syrup.

Egg Salad

In the spring, after dyeing eggs for Easter, we always have plenty of hard-boiled eggs in need of transformation. This recipe is for a basic egg salad. Once you have mastered it, try adding other ingredients such as diced celery, diced onions, diced pickles, a bit of curry powder, chopped walnuts, fresh herbs, or dried cranberries. Let your culinary imagination shine!

SERVES 4

INGREDIENTS

- 8 hard-boiled eggs, peeled
- ½ cup mayonnaise
- Pickle relish or chopped celery (optional)
- Salt and pepper
- Sandwich bread

Instructions

1. Dice the eggs on a cutting board and put into a medium bowl.

2. Add the mayonnaise, relish, and a sprinkle of salt and pepper and mix well.

3. Spread onto sandwich bread and enjoy.

Deviled Eggs

Here's a tasty way to use up a surplus of eggs. Deviled eggs are fun to make and even more fun to eat — you have to use your fingers with these messy treats. This is a basic recipe that you can add your favorite mix-ins to. Try bacon bits, pickle relish, hot sauce, or finely chopped onion, for example.

MAKES 16 EGGS

INGREDIENTS

- 8 hard-boiled eggs
- 4 tablespoons mayonnaise
- 1 teaspoon brown mustard
- 1 teaspoon red wine vinegar
- Salt and pepper
- Garnish (optional, but try paprika or chopped chives)

Instructions

1. Peel the eggs and carefully slice them in half lengthwise.

2. Scoop the yolks into a medium bowl and set the whites on a platter.

3. Mash the yolks with the mayonnaise, mustard, and vinegar until creamy. Add salt and pepper to taste.

4. Spoon the filling back into the egg whites. Garnish as desired.

Egg Drop Soup

Our family loves eating at Chinese restaurants. We always start off with a bowl of egg drop soup, and we like it so much we started making it at home. This soup comes together in no time, and it's so much fun pouring the eggs through the fork!

SERVES 4

INGREDIENTS

32	ounces chicken broth
2	tablespoons soy sauce
1	tablespoon fresh ginger paste
4	scallions, diced
3	eggs
1	tablespoon cornstarch

Instructions

1. Put the chicken broth, soy sauce, ginger, and scallions in a stockpot on the stove. Bring to a boil over medium-high heat, then turn it down to a simmer.

2. In the meantime, crack the eggs into a small bowl and whisk them well. Set them aside.

3. Add the cornstarch to a small bowl and then pour in ½ cup of the broth. Whisk together until all the lumps are gone. Pour the mixture into the pot.

4. Stir the eggs up with a fork, then slowly pour them into the simmering soup through the fork, stirring in between. They will cook almost immediately, forming whitish streaks, and your soup is ready to eat!

Mexican Egg Pizza

Our whole family looks forward to pizza and a movie on Friday nights. We make several different types of pizza, but our most creative one is this Mexican egg pizza. How cool is it to have fried eggs on top of pizza?

SERVES 4

INGREDIENTS

1	premade pizza crust or ball of dough
	Cooking spray
	Tomato salsa
1	cup grated cheddar cheese
1	cup grated Monterey Jack cheese
4–6	eggs
	Avocado slices
	Fresh chopped cilantro

Instructions

1. Preheat the oven to 400°F/205°C. Spray a cookie sheet or pizza pan with cooking spray.

2. Spread the pizza dough on the sheet and bake for 5 minutes.

3. Spread a thin layer of salsa over the crust and sprinkle with the cheeses.

4. Carefully crack the eggs onto the pizza, leaving about an inch between them. Try not to break the yolks.

5. Bake for 8 to 10 minutes, until the crust and cheese begin to brown and the eggs are cooked through.

6. Top with avocado and cilantro.

Bacon, Spinach & Cheese Quiche

The wonderful thing about quiche is that you can serve it for any meal. It is fun to be creative and add a variety of ingredients to the basic quiche recipe. I hope you will try this one, and try substituting other meats, vegetables, and cheeses to make new recipes for your family to enjoy.

SERVES 4

INGREDIENTS

- 1 premade piecrust
- 6 eggs
- ½ cup milk
- 1 cup shredded cheddar cheese
- ½ cup (2–3 slices) cooked, crumbled bacon
- ½ cup cooked spinach, squeezed to remove excess moisture and chopped

Instructions

1. Preheat the oven to 350°F/175°C.

2. Line a pie pan with the piecrust and set it aside.

3. Whisk the eggs and milk in a mixing bowl until they are well combined.

4. Stir the cheese, bacon, and spinach into the egg mixture.

5. Pour the egg mixture into the piecrust.

6. Bake for approximately 40 minutes.

7. Insert a toothpick into the center of the quiche to check for doneness. If it comes out clean, the quiche is done. Let the quiche sit on the counter for about 10 minutes before serving.

CREATE YOUR OWN QUICHE

Here are some other tasty combinations that you can try.

½ cup your choice of meats:

- → Bacon
- → Chicken, cooked and shredded
- → Ground beef, cooked
- → Ham, cooked and cubed

1 cup your choice of cheeses:

- → Blue cheese crumbles
- → Cheddar, grated
- → Feta
- → Mozzarella
- → Swiss

½ cup vegetables:

- → Carrots, shredded
- → Celery, diced
- → Kale, chopped
- → Leeks, chopped
- → Olives
- → Spinach, chopped
- → Tomatoes, diced

French-Style Fresh Berry Clafouti

My kids love this dish for the name alone: *klah-foo-TEE*. Try saying that five times fast! Kind of like a flan, a custard, and a soufflé mixed together, clafouti is traditionally made with cherries, but you can use peaches, berries, pears, or apricots. This easy, versatile dish makes a lovely dessert, especially with a scoop of vanilla ice cream. Clafouti also makes a healthy breakfast!

SERVES 6

INGREDIENTS

2 tablespoons butter, melted
5 eggs
1 cup sugar
1¼ cups light cream
1½ tablespoons vanilla extract
A good pinch of salt
¾ cup flour
2 cups mixed berries
Confectioners' sugar

Instructions

1. Preheat the oven to 375°F/190°C. Coat the bottom and the sides of a 7- by 11-inch baking pan with the butter.

2. Whisk the eggs, sugar, cream, vanilla, and salt thoroughly in a mixing bowl. Add the flour and mix until smooth.

3. Wash the berries and dry them. Blueberries, blackberries, and raspberries can be left whole, but cut strawberries in half.

4. Pour the egg mixture into the baking dish. Scatter the berries evenly on top of the egg mixture.

5. Bake for approximately 40 minutes, until the top edges are golden brown, and a knife inserted into the center comes out clean. Don't open the oven door while the clafouti is baking, to allow it to properly rise.

6. Dust with confectioners' sugar and serve warm.

Custard-Style Rice Pudding

Puddings are one of my family's favorite desserts. I love sharing my childhood recipes with my kids, and this one is based on one that my mother used to make for me. Of course, we mixed it up a bit and added a couple of eggs to make this rice pudding even creamier and more delicious.

SERVES 4–6

INGREDIENTS

Butter
½ cup uncooked rice
4 cups milk
2 eggs
1 (14-ounce) can sweetened condensed milk
1 teaspoon salt
½ teaspoon ground cinnamon
½ teaspoon ground nutmeg
½ cup raisins (optional)
Whipped cream, for serving

Instructions

1. Preheat the oven to 325°F/165°C. Grease a 2-quart baking dish with butter.

2. Combine the rice and 2 cups of the milk in a saucepan and bring to a low simmer. Cook, stirring occasionally, until the rice is soft, approximately 20 minutes. Remove the pan from the heat and set it aside.

3. Whisk the remaining 2 cups of milk, eggs, sweetened condensed milk, salt, cinnamon, nutmeg, and raisins in a large bowl until thoroughly combined. Stir in the rice and milk mixture.

4. Pour the mixture into the baking dish and place it on the center rack in the oven. Bake for approximately 50 minutes, until slightly brown around the edges. Stir once at the 20-minute mark.

5. Serve warm or chilled topped with whipped cream. Store unused portion in the refrigerator.

RESOURCES

Your local feed store is always a great resource. However, if you need more help, try the organizations listed here. You'll find all kinds of information on these websites and can order almost anything you might need. Here are some good general websites to start with:

BackYard Chickens
www.backyardchickens.com

The Livestock Conservancy
919-542-5704
www.livestockconservancy.org

My Pet Chicken
888-460-1529
www.mypetchicken.com

Hatcheries

Cackle Hatchery
417-532-4581
www.cacklehatchery.com

Dunlap Hatchery
208-459-9088
www.dunlaphatchery.net

Ideal Poultry Breeding Farms, Inc.
254-697-6677
www.idealpoultry.com

Meyer Hatchery
888-568-9755
www.meyerhatchery.com

Mt. Healthy Hatcheries
800-451-5603
www.mthealthy.com

Murray McMurray Hatchery
800-456-3280
www.mcmurrayhatchery.com

Smith Poultry & Game Bird Supply
913-879-2587
www.poultrysupplies.com

Coops and Supplies

ChickenWaterer.com
408-239-3026
www.chickenwaterer.com

Chubby Mealworms
855-473-6592
www.chubbymealworms.com

Happy Hen Treats
www.happyhentreats.com

Horizon Structures
888-447-4337
www.horizonstructures.com

Louise's Country Closet
www.louisescountrycloset.com
Hen saddles

Manna Pro
800-690-9908
www.mannapro.com

Nite Guard
800-328-6647
www.niteguard.com

Randall Burkey Company
800-531-1097
www.randallburkey.com

Treats for Chickens
707-664-8124
www.treatsforchickens.com

Poultry Showing

American Poultry Association (APA)
724-729-3459
www.amerpoultryassn.com

National 4-H Council
www.4-h.org

Poultry Show Central
www.poultryshowcentral.com

INDEX

MORE STOREY BOOKS FOR CHICKEN LOVERS

Barnyard Games & Puzzles by Helene Hovanec & Patrick Merrell
Country kids and city kids alike will enjoy the variety of games centered around barnyard life. For children ages 6 to 10.
144 pages. Paper. ISBN 978-1-58017-630-9.

Chick Days by Jenna Woginrich; photography by Mars Vilaubi
A delightful photographic guide for absolute beginners, chronicling the journey of three chickens from newly hatched to fully grown.
128 pages. Paper. ISBN 978-1-60342-584-1.

The Chicken Encyclopedia by Gail Damerow
From albumen to zygote, the terminology of everything chicken is demystified.
320 pages. Paper. ISBN 978-1-60342-561-2.

Chicken Games & Puzzles by Helene Hovanec & Patrick Merrell
These chicken-themed challenges are adorably illustrated and give hours of fun. For children ages 6 to 9.
144 pages. Paper. ISBN 978-1-61212-087-4.

Pocketful of Poultry by Carol Ekarius
More than 100 amazing poultry pals in full-page color photographs.
272 pages. Paper. ISBN 978-1-58017-677-4.

Pop-Out & Paint Farm Animals by Cindy A. Littlefield
Make a barnyard full of 26 standup animals, from cows and roosters to pigs and sheep, using the sturdy pop-out templates included and the step-by-step photos of how to paint each one. For children ages 8 to 12.
48 pages plus 20 die-cut cards. Paper. ISBN 978-1-61212-139-0.

These and other books from Storey Publishing are available
wherever quality books are sold or by calling 1-800-441-5700.
Visit us at *www.storey.com* or sign up for our newsletter
at *www.storey.com/signup*.